Consult Your Inner Psychic

Consult Your
Inner Psychic

HOW TO USE INTUITIVE GUIDANCE
TO MAKE YOUR LIFE WORK BETTER

CAROLE LYNNE

WEISER BOOKS
Boston, MA/York Beach, ME

First published in 2005 by
Red Wheel/Weiser, LLC
York Beach, ME
With offices at:
368 Congress Street
Boston, MA 02210
www.redwheelweiser.com

Library of Congress Cataloging-in-Publication Data
Lynne, Carole.
Consult your inner psychic : how to use intuitive guidance to
make your life work better / Carole Lynne.
p. cm.
ISBN 1-57863-343-5 (alk. paper)
1. Decision making—Psychic aspects. 2. Intuition. I. Title.
BF1045.D42L96 2005
133.8—dc22   2005009146

Typeset in Sabon by Sky Peck Design
Printed in the United States
Malloy

12 11 10 09 08 07 06 05
8   7   6   5   4   3   2   1
The paper used in this publication meets the minimum requirements of the
American National Standard for Information Sciences—Permanence of Paper
for Printed Library Materials Z39.48-1992 (R1997).

*I dedicate this book and my life
to my wonderful husband
Marlowe Teig,
a man whose spiritual qualities
come to him so naturally.*

Contents

CD Contents

Four States of Being Meditation (20:01)
The Observer (2:57)
The Soloist (3:14)
The Producer (3:27)
The Voter (3:13)
The Warrior (3:33)
The Nurturer (2:57)
The Seeker (2:24)
The Communicator (3:19)
The Lover (3:01)
The Peacemaker (3:15)
The Devotee (2:45)
The Healer (2:46)

Foreword

WHETHER YOU REALIZE IT OR NOT, you are constantly being guided—we all are. It doesn't matter what name you give to this guiding source. You can call it God, the Universe, Infinite Spirit, Higher Self, spirit guides, angels, source, or energy. I tend to prefer the term spirit guides, but naming this guiding source is not what's important. What is important is that you have an awareness that it exists. Once you are aware of this guidance, you can learn how to utilize it as an empowering tool for making choices and navigating your way toward a happier, healthier, and even wealthier life. This book teaches us how to retrieve that guidance using a simple, systematic method. And it is one of the most direct and powerful tools I have used.

Six years ago, I was a cynical, narrow-minded skeptic. At that time, I didn't believe that there were people who could communicate with spirits. And I certainly didn't believe that I had any intuitive abilities myself. It wasn't until I met my first legitimate psychic medium and received indisputable messages from my deceased father and grandmother that I became a believer. That's when I began my journey researching the afterlife and getting readings from more than one hundred gifted psychic mediums around the globe.

It took a long time for me to go from skeptic to believer, but by doing the research and proving to myself that all this was true, I was able to make the transition. After gathering a plethora of evidence that psychic mediums truly can communicate with people on the other side, I became a knower. I now *know* that the spirit world exists, that people can communicate with spirits, and that our lives are guided by people in spirit known as spirit guides.

Once I finally got over the hurdle of my skepticism, I learned how psychic mediums communicate with the spirit world. The truth is that it is all about energetic vibration. Mediums have learned to raise the energetic vibration of their minds so that people in spirit can lower their energetic vibration, thereby creating a link between the two. This link allows them to transfer information such as thoughts, sounds, sights, even telepathic pictures and feelings.

The next thing I learned is that our spirit guides communicate with us constantly without us needing to raise our own vibration. The fact is that they always know what we are saying, doing, and thinking, so their only challenge is in getting us to know what they are communicating to us in order to guide us. They do this through our intuition, gut feelings, and hunches.

This insight taught me that while professional psychic mediums can help us to receive messages more directly from our spirit guides, we don't necessarily need a medium to communicate with our guides. We simply need to learn how to interpret what our guides are communicating to us via our intuition. This is an empowering idea because once we become aware of our psychic intuitive guidance and learn to make use of it on our own, we won't have to rely upon others to do it for us.

While consulting a psychic medium can be extremely helpful in some cases, there are two problems with relying on psychic mediums for ongoing guidance. The first is that there is always room for misinterpretation. My experience is that, once we have learned how to access our intuitive guidance on our own, we are always more accurate at interpreting our own intuitive messages than anyone else could possibly be doing it for us. The second problem with being dependent upon a psychic medium for guidance is that, depending on your circumstances, contacting a medium whenever you need guidance might be inconvenient, costly, or unfeasible.

In *Consult Your Inner Psychic*, Carole Lynne, one of the mediums I recommend on my website *BestPsychicMediums.com*, teaches people how to identify and interpret psychic intuitive guidance without the help of a psychic medium. To write a book that teaches your clients how to do what you do for them, thereby training them to no longer need your services, is a true act of integrity. It reminds me of the old adage, "Give a man a fish and he'll eat for a day. Teach a man to fish and he'll eat for a lifetime." Carole Lynne teaches you to connect with your psychic intuitive guidance so you don't have to get a reading from a professional every time you have a question. It is an invaluable ability that will be yours forever.

What you're about to learn in the chapters that follow is nothing short of extraordinary. I know because I've given myself readings using the process taught in this book with incredible success. And I've noticed that as time goes on, I find myself returning to it again and again. I never considered myself very intuitive until I learned this process. Perhaps it is the accompanying CD that helps me to tune my mind for optimal intuitive vibration. All I know for sure is that I now trust my intuition like never before. And, for me, that confidence is empowering.

Learning to connect with your inner guidance provides you with a priceless roadmap toward achieving everything you want to have, be, or do in life. It is not enough that we pray or send our intentions out into the Universe. We must also be aware of the guidance that comes in response to our prayers and intentions. Otherwise we know the desired destination but not the path for getting there. By reading *Consult Your Inner Psychic* and practicing the system it provides, you will forever have a tool for obtaining the direction you've requested.

Congratulations on attracting this book and CD into your life!

—BOB OLSON

Founder of *BestPsychicMediums.com*

and editor of *OfSpirit.com* magazine

Acknowledgments

I WOULD LIKE TO GIVE HEARTFELT THANKS to all those who have helped in the production of this book and CD.

First of all I would like to thank Nat Hefferman, who worked alongside me composing the music for the CD and who also engineered all the recording sessions. Nat is a very creative and patient person and I could not have completed the CD without him.

I would like to thank Cindy Williamson, Christine McGeever, Bob Blake, and Bill Shevlin, who worked with the psychic intuitive guidance process as it unfolded. The comments from the "users" of the book and CD helped me enormously as we discovered how the process helped each person who worked with the messages and the music.

My thanks goes to all those in my life who have encouraged me to listen to my own inner voice. I am fortunate to have many people in my life who practice inner listening and therefore are a great support to me in my everyday life and my work. I specifically want to thank all those in the meditation group I sit with as well as my students.

I would like to thank those in the world of spirit who help me retrieve my own psychic intuitive guidance, because while my conscious mind gave me the words for the beginning chapters, the Twelve Energies, the Four States of Being, the Messages, and the words for the meditation on the CD were all retrieved from that other part of my being that receives intuitive guidance.

Thank you to Joseph Campbell, Caroline Myss, and Wayne Dyer. I appreciate the incredible work they have done in their books to educate me and to motivate me to be the best person I can be. My trips to southern and northern India, England, Scotland, and the Hawaiian Islands have also given me many experiences that have influenced both my writing and composing. The singing bowl, the Indian Struthie, and drums all added to the textures of the music. The musicians I have listened to and met in these countries all contribute to the vocal sounds that flow through me.

My deepest gratitude goes to my publisher, Jan Johnson, and to Jill Rogers who has overseen the editing of all my books.

Note to Readers

THE PSYCHIC INTUITIVE GUIDANCE PROCESS described herein is meant to supplement, not be a substitute for, professional medical care or treatment. There are serious situations in life where we need to get the help of the medical community or a psychological counselor, and we encourage all readers to use common sense and get the help they need. Neither the author nor the publisher accepts any responsibility for your health or how you choose to use the process in this book.

YOU HAVE THE ANSWERS

How often have you said, "You know, I saw that coming"? Hindsight can be devastating. Especially when you look back at a situation and wish you had handled it in a different way. Mysteriously, a part of your consciousness *knew* exactly what you needed to do, and yet you did something else. And as you look back you say, "You know, I saw that coming, but I did not listen. I had a gut feeling and I did not follow it. I had a hunch and decided my feelings were silly. If only I had paid attention to my gut reaction." This is your story, and this is my story. If we can learn to listen to our psychic intuitive guidance, our lives can be totally transformed.

The Psychic Intuitive Guidance Process is a tool for accessing your own inner wisdom. The answers are within you, and this process can help create an emotional, psychological, and spiritual environment in which you are able to hear your inner wisdom. You will be forever changed by the experiences you have with this process. While you will consult with experts and friends when needed, you will have more trust in your own ability to solve problems and live a positive life.

I call this a "psychic" process, because it relates to the soul and the inner wisdom each one of us can access. The original use of the word *psychic* related to the soul, and that is how I am using the word. I use the word *intuitive* because it is intuition that each one of us will use as we work with this process. I use the word *guidance* because we will be accessing the guidance of our inner wisdom, which is ultimately connected to the Creator of All That Exists.

I have written this book and, along with Nat Hefferman, created the accompanying CD because I want to share what I have learned with you. This book and CD are tools that will facilitate your process of going within and listening to your inner wisdom. You will experience the mystery and vitality of the Twelve Energies and acquire the flexibility to move in and out of situations using the Four States of Being. There are messages to read and music to listen to that will help you get what you need. Psychic Intuitive Guidance is an easy-to-learn, easy-to-understand, enjoyable process for improving your life. Learn to use this tool of empowerment and give yourself the opportunity to manage your life in the moment, every moment.

PART I

The Psychic Intuitive
Guidance Process

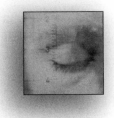

Chapter 1

YOUR INNER PSYCHIC

In this day and age, when life seems to be moving so fast, and there are so many experts giving us conflicting opinions about what to do, it is imperative that we learn how to cope with the continual changes and barrage of opinions our fast-paced lives present. Ultimately, each one of us is responsible for our own life, and we have to make our own choices. Many of us give our power away to others and let other people run our lives because it has become too difficult to cope with the confusion we feel inside. But life is changing every moment, and we need to learn to manage our responses to all that happens.

Would you like to be in a good mood more of the time, no matter what is happening? Would you like to make better choices each year, each day, each second? Would you like to limit the amount of time that you are angry, worried, frantic, or depressed? Then I invite you to learn about and work with the Psychic Intuitive Guidance Process.

I used to be upset and aggravated a great deal of the time because I could not cope with the many changes in life that would occur: changes as small as hearing that an appointment had been moved up an hour and as large as hearing about the passing on of a loved one. Large or small, change always threw me off, and I had a terrible time with it. I was not a totally unhappy person, but I wasted a great deal of energy feeling upset and out of control until I learned to listen to my psychic intuitive guidance and learned how to deal with change in a more positive way.

A Spiritual Connection

Using your psychic intuitive guidance is a spiritual process. Why? Because in order to manage change well, each one of us needs to get in touch with the inner guide that is connected to the Divine. There is a part of each one of us that is connected to Divine consciousness. People use many words to describe what is nearly indescribable: God, Infinite Spirit, Nature, Universal Harmony, the Creator of All That Is, the Divine, or the Supreme Being. You may have your own way of describing what I am calling the Creator of All That Is. I believe that this Divine energy is what has created life and continues to create life each second. The universe is a constant and ongoing miracle. The power that has created the universe continues to create it each second.

We Come from Different Backgrounds
I know that each of you who reads this book and listens to the CD may come from a different religious background. And some of you may choose not to be part of any organized religion. While we do not all perceive God in the same way, I do know that there is a still and quiet voice that speaks within each one of us. We call that voice by different names. We have many different opinions

about what that voice is and where it comes from. It is not my wish to try to convince anyone to think the same way I do. While I share my spiritual perspective with you, I respect that you may have a different point of view. All that we need to agree on is that there *is* a voice that speaks to us. I call that voice "the voice of inner wisdom."

In my belief, each of us is part of that Divine energy, and when we are able to tune in to and listen to the guidance of the Divine within each of us, we make better choices for our lives. Deep within, we know what to do, but often we do not listen to our inner selves.

Each Moment Is Its Own Guidance

I have read countless books on managing one's life. I have tried to manage my life with all kinds of logically based systems. I have read books about time management, diet, exercise, and all kinds of other self-improvement. These books and courses have been wonderful and have helped me to a certain degree. But though they gave great suggestions and "answers" to my problems, the suggested solutions often felt inadequate. I realized that while everything I learned in logically based systems was helpful, something was missing.

When I began to unfold spiritually, I started to let go of the layers of defense that separated me from the Creator. My life began to change, and the way I approached challenges in my life also changed. As I accepted that part of myself that is connected to the Creator, I began to listen to the psychic intuitive voice of guidance that speaks directly to me. What I have learned through spiritual unfoldment is that there *is* no answer. Each moment in life carries its own challenges, and what we need to do in each moment has to be determined *in that moment*. We need to tune into our inner wisdom for guidance. The answer that may have worked twenty minutes ago may not be valid for this moment.

There are times when an inner voice of wisdom speaks to us and tells us what is best in this moment. But do we listen?

Now, bear with me for a moment. I am not suggesting that you change your mind every twenty minutes about where to live, whom to be married to, or other long-term decisions. Yes, there are answers that remain the same, but as we live each moment of our lives, life keeps changing, and we have to respond to the moment. And even those "long-term" decisions need to be reviewed occasionally to see if they decisions still make sense in the present moment.

The Psychic Intuitive Guidance Process

There are many things that I am not good at. I cannot fix your kitchen sink, fill out your tax forms, or repair your car. But I can teach you how to live a better and happier life. I am able to teach people to do things in a manner that is easily understandable, easy to learn, and easy to carry out. So if you will allow me to be your coach, I will teach you a process of relating to life that I believe will improve the quality of your life every day. You will be in a better mood; you will be more successful in everything you do. You will find that you can more easily deal with every bend and curve that life brings you. You will have peace of mind.

As your coach through this process, my goals for you are the following:

- You will quickly learn to use this process and then have a creative spiritual tool to make your life work better right now.

- You will listen to your psychic intuitive guidance instead of believing that somebody else always has better advice for you.

- You will own your power instead of giving it away to others.

- You will make better moment-to-moment decisions.

- You will be able to alter your current mood quickly, within three seconds to thirty minutes.

- You will be able to make better choices, both short term and long term.

- You will have fun using this process and be inspired to adapt this method, as needed, to make it your own.

Learning the Psychic Intuitive Guidance Process

I am realistic about the fact that people do not all learn the same way, and I have provided two approaches for learning this process: the Quick Start Approach and the Slow and Steady Approach. For those of you who cannot wait to use the process, read the overview of the process in chapter 4. Then once you have tried the process, go back and read the rest of the chapters in part 1. For those of you who have more patience, read all of the chapters in part 1 before working with the process.

Before you proceed with either approach, read the following bird's-eye view of the Psychic Intuitive Guidance Process as it is laid out in this book:

1. Part 1 presents the tools of the process—the Twelve Energies, the Four States of Being, the forty-eight messages, and the CD of meditations and archetypal music. You will also learn how to give yourself an intuitive reading:

- Ask a question about your life.

- Ask, "Which of the Twelve Energies do I need in this moment?" (The Twelve Energies are discussed in chapter 5.)

- Ask, "Which of the Four States of Being do I need to apply to the Energy I have chosen?" (The Four States of Being are covered in chapter 6.)

- Now you have an Energy-State of Being Combination.

2. Part 2 contains the messages that you will read as you listen to tracks on the CD. The combination of the message and the music will help you access your psychic intuitive guidance.

- Say you have chosen the Energy-State of Being Combination of "The Lover-Retreating From." Turn to page 67 for the beginning of a list of the messages included in part 2. Find the page number of the message for "The Lover-Retreating From" on the list.

- Now turn to that page, and notice the number of the CD track at the top of the page.

- Start playing the designated track on your CD player while you read the message silently or out loud. Notice how you react to the experience of reading the message and listening to the music. How does the experience relate to the question you asked?

3. In part 3 you will receive instruction on how to get the most out of your experience with the Psychic Intuitive Guidance Process. You will learn how to use this process with a friend or with me or another professional intuitive reader. Stories about the experiences of others with the process serve as examples that you can learn from.

My life has changed and is still changing as I continue to use the Psychic Intuitive Guidance Process, and I am very excited and eager to share it with you.

Are you ready?

Let's get started.

Chapter 2

THE HAPPINESS TRAIN
IS LEAVING THE STATION

As you start working with the Psychic Intuitive Guidance Process, the first thing you need to do is to get on the "happiness train."

Those of us who have made a commitment to being more positive and happier people are on that train. If you are not on that train, it is going to leave without you. These may sound like tough words, but I truly believe that it is your choice (and it is my choice) to be happy or unhappy.

There was a time I felt truly sorry for people, but not any more. I have great compassion for people who are struggling with difficult challenges. But my days of feeling sorry for others, when they do nothing to improve their lives, is over. I have seen too many people with incredible disabilities who live extremely positive and happy lives to be able to feel sorry for the average person who is wallowing in their problems. There are people who cannot walk, talk, or who have other extremely difficult challenges who are happier and more positive than some of the rich and spoiled people who complain about everything they can find.

It is not that I do not have compassion for people experiencing serious medical depression. We need to do everything we can to get such people to receive the vital medical help they need. However, the greater percentages of us who are unhappy are not medically depressed. *We are negligent.* We are not taking responsibility for our own happiness. So get on the happiness train of thinking *now,* and be happier *now.*

Get Rid of the "As Soon As" Mentality!

Many people live by the "as soon as" mentality. I do not deserve to be overly critical, as I have lived years enveloped by this mentality. Now that I am out of it, I want to shout for joy and identify this mentality for you, so that if you are "captured" by it you can free yourself. I also encourage you to free yourself from others who are infected with this negative mentality.

The "As Soon As" Mentality

As soon as I lose ten pounds, I will feel happy. As soon as I clean out the garage, I will feel better.

As soon as:

- I find a new love relationship

- The kids are in school

- The kids are out of school

- I am on vacation

- I find a new job

- I quit this job

- I get over this cold

- I get a good report on my medical tests

- I have a beautiful home

- My son visits me from college

- My daughter comes home

- My mother passes and I do not have to take care of her

- I get married

- I get divorced

- This snowstorm is over

- It snows and we can go skiing

- This heat wave passes

- This chilly spell is over

- These house guests leave

- My company arrives

- I have house trained my pet

- I have toilet trained my child

- As soon as soon as soon as soon as

Let's face it: Things will never be perfect. Yes, there will be perfect moments, maybe even perfect hours and days. But the "as soon as" mentality that many people live with saps their energy, and they are never happy.

Be Happy Now

All of us could be happy nearly every day if we stopped waiting until something else happens. Of course we will be satisfied when certain things have happened, but if we base our contentment in life on what is going to happen in the future, we will *never* be happy, because once the future arrives, there will be a whole new list of conditions that have to be met before we can be content. *Living to be happy as soon as something happens is a pathway to unhappiness.*

It goes without saying that when real tragedy strikes, we are not going to be able to be happy every moment. When a loved one passes on to the eternal world, we are going to grieve. When you or I or any of our loved ones becomes ill, we are going to be anxious. However, some of the happiest people I know are people who are suffering through great problems and have still found ways to value every moment of their lives.

I have a friend who has cancer. The doctors tell her she has a short time to live, and she says, "Nonsense." She has already lived past most of the predicted times of her passing. Yes, she is doing everything possible to settle her affairs, but she is not living each day in dread of passing. She is living her life; she is reading, writing, and entertaining friends.

On the other hand, the other day, when I met a woman on the beach at a hotel in Kihei, on Maui, all she did was complain. She complained that the surf was too high on the beach we were standing on, and every time she went in the water she got sand in her bathing suit.

She complained about the fact that she had just come down to the hotel pool and the beach chairs were still wet. I looked at the ocean and found it to be one of the most wonderful sights in the world. I looked at the beach chairs wet with the morning dew and thought about how fortunate I was to be outside without a jacket, when people on the East Coast were having zero degree weather. The woman went on complaining for a long time. I looked at her face and could see that the lines of a frown were beginning to be etched in her face. Frankly, I felt compassion for her, because she had such a huge set of expectations that had to be met. Her day was already ruined, and it was only nine in the morning.

Now, in all fairness to this woman, perhaps she and her husband had spent thousands of dollars to take a trip to Hawaii, and she was disappointed when everything did not live up to her expectations of a "fantasy vacation." But the truth is, most experiences in life are not as we envision them. To enjoy life, we have to be ready to enjoy whatever happens and do whatever is necessary to make the best of every opportunity that life gives us, sunny or rainy.

The fantasy vacation and the fantasy life do not exist!

I planned many fantasy vacations that never turned out to be the way I had expected them to be. The weather was not what it was supposed to be, my body was not as beautiful and as thin as it was supposed to be, my husband was not in as good a mood as he was supposed to be, and on and on and on. Somehow, vacations and other events that I took such care to plan exactly did not unfold as I had wanted. Yes, I was disappointed, but as I learn to listen to my inner wisdom, those negative feelings become few and farther between.

An Omelet with an Attitude

Here is a story of something that happened to me that made me realize I had really changed my attitude. It is a story about making an omelet. Sometimes a simple experience can be life changing, as it brings us an opportunity to look at life in a more positive and creative manner.

Almost every morning I make an omelet for myself. I use liquid egg substitutes, leftover green vegetables from last night's dinner, and a bit of low-fat cheese. I have to get all my ingredients set up right, because as those of you who make omelets know, timing is everything.

One morning as I was making my omelet, I did not execute the timing correctly. I poured the eggs into the pan too soon, and it was sort of an "egg mush" situation. When I tried to pull the edges of the omelet into the center, they stuck. This infuriated me. "Damn frying pan," I screamed at my husband, who looked up momentarily from his paper and quickly went back to it, as he knew what was coming. Well, my rhetoric that began with the damn frying pan evolved into focusing on problems I have had my entire life. One hour later I was still complaining and had barely finished eating my omelet, which had come out looking like shredded Styrofoam.

Enter the transformed omelet. On another morning, I made the same mistake in timing, but *this* morning I was in a creative mood: ready to take on the world no matter what. The omelet stuck to the side of the pan, but instead of becoming irritable, I became challenged by the situation. I very carefully tried to pull the edges of the omelet into the center, and it worked. Then when it was time to flip over one half of the omelet onto itself, the flip did not work. The omelet was tearing. But I starting flipping whatever parts of the omelet would flip, and I ended up with an omelet in the form of a triangle. I was stunned. It was beautiful. If I had tried my hardest I could never have created an omelet that looked like this one.

Many of the great discoveries in our world have been made when someone took advantage of what seemed like a mistake. While I do not mean to imply that my triangle omelet was in any way a great discovery, it *was* a great transforming moment for me. This moment displayed for me how different life is when I am in a creative and positive mood. It showed me how to make lemonade out of lemons and a triangle omelet out of what could have been just a mess of eggs.

Get on the Happiness Train and Travel Light!

I ask that you decide right now to have a more positive attitude toward whatever happens in life. As we work together with the Psychic Intuitive Guidance Process, it is your positive attitude that will make this process work for you. Choose to see the glass half-full instead of half-empty. Your life will start working better, right now.

If you have serious problems, see a therapist and join a support group so that you have a designated time and place to cope with your problems in a positive and professional manner. Do not carry those problems around with you every minute of every day. Do not ruin your family relationships and other close relationships by spending all your time complaining and processing your problems. Life is too short.

You can look at life as simply wonderful or you can look at life as complex and impossible. Life will honor your thinking by being exactly the way you see it. Remember:

- Give up the "as soon as" mentality.

- Decide to be happy now.

- Get on the happiness train and travel light.

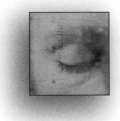

Chapter 3

ALL IS CHANGE

All of life is changing every second. Nothing stays the same, ever.

As we understand that each of us is a part of the consciousness and vibration of the universe, we can begin to take advantage of the incredible opportunities that are available every second. While we may be challenged by the fact that life is always changing, this fact also provides for greater movement and flexibility, if we can avoid resisting change.

Change is all that is, ever was, and ever will be. As we realize that nothing stays the same, we can ask ourselves an important question: "If everything is changing, why bother trying to control life so much?" Life is simply uncontrollable. Of course, on one level there are many things we *can* control in life. We may stay in the same living space, with the same partner, work at the same job, and spend time with the same friends. But then something happens called "a change," and if it is something that we had not planned for, we fall apart. Our bubble is burst, and we become unhappy.

We do not have to be unhappy if we understand that the underlying reality of existence is change. The God of your understanding has created this ever-changing universe. And whatever that power is that has created this universe continues to create it every moment. As we accept the reality of the ever-changing and moving universe, we can be closer to the truth of existence and therefore closer to the Creator.

With this Divine knowledge, life will never look the same again. It is my personal belief that Divine Consciousness is what many people call God, and that this essence flows within each one of us and through all that exists in the universe. Everything that exists is part of the flowing, vibrating, ever-changing energy of the universe. With the acceptance of change comes the acceptance of yourself and others, the acceptance of all the cycles of life from season to season and from birth to maturity to aging and death.

In a changing universe, the answers are also changing. Each one of us must check in often with our psychic intuitive guidance because, just like all of existence, the answers are changing. What worked five minutes ago may not be the best solution in *this* moment. There is a deeper part of us, connected to the Divine that knows what is best in this moment, if we will only listen.

The happiest people I know cope effectively with change. They are able to live in the moment. This does not mean that they are scatterbrains changing direction every time the wind blows. They have plans and commitments. But they also tune into their intuition so that they know when to change plans. They know whether a total reorganization is needed or whether the current plan simply needs to be tweaked a bit.

Nancy runs a small company, and she has a business plan. Things are going well, but she notices that sales have been down for the past three months. Nancy copes with change by offering a sale on a couple of popular items, and she reduces her expenses by laying off one employee and working longer hours herself. She may not be happy about the layoff, but it is critical to her staying in business. If she goes out of business, she and ten other people will not have jobs. Nancy is coping effectively with change.

Bob is in love with a woman named Judy, and Judy is not taking their relationship as seriously as is Bob. In fact, Judy is seeing another man as well as spending time with Bob, even though she has told Bob he is the only person she is dating. Bob finds out about Judy's other dates and becomes depressed. But Bob, who cares about being happy, only allows himself to be depressed for a couple of days. As he tunes into his inner guidance, he knows what he has to do. He calls Judy and tells her that as much as he cares for her, it is too painful to continue to date her while she is dating other people. He tells Judy that because she has lied to him, he can no longer trust her, and it is time for him to say good-bye. Bob plans a vacation within the next few months that he can look forward to and goes on with his life. Bob is coping effectively with change.

Unsuccessful people use change to add to their unhappiness. Jane is redecorating her house. She has a house painting company lined up to paint and wallpaper most of the rooms in her house within eight weeks. She is happy about the start and finish dates because her cousins are coming to visit from Europe in ten weeks and Jane wants the work to be completed before they arrive.

Change happens! The house painting company manager calls Jane the day before they are to start the work and says that there has been a death in the family of their most important worker, and they cannot start the painting and wallpapering project for a month. Jane goes into a spin. She is frantic. She is clearly out of control, so much that she is not paying attention to where she is going when she starts down the stairs to the basement, and she falls down the stairs and breaks her leg. Now, she is totally dev-astated and absolutely sure that the universe is out to get her.

If Jane had been able to stop and tune into her intuitive guid-ance, she might have understood that she had many choices:

- She could try to find another company to do the job in her time frame.

- She could arrange with her visitors to stay with her at a different time.

- She could go see the visitors in Europe instead of having them visit her.

Any one of us could think of many options that Jane could have acted upon if only she had listened to her intuitive guidance instead of getting herself into a frenzy. To make things worse, she was thinking only of herself when she reacted to the bad news, and she had no compassion for the worker who had a death in his family.

Beware of "Expert" Advice

We live in an age in which there are many people telling us how we can be healthier, live longer, be more successful, and be better looking. In fact, no matter what the decision—what car to buy, how to fix a leak under the sink, making major health decisions—there are people to tell us how to do it! Some who are telling us what to do are really experts in their field, while others with lim-ited knowledge and a good marketing plan are presenting them-selves as experts. There are people from every corner of the world and corner of the street, ready to tell us how to live. *Who should we believe?*

In this day and age it seems like research studies can be found to back up any expert in anything. Daily we hear about new medical and psychological studies from "the experts." As one study disagrees with the next, many of us are left confused and bewildered. There was a time when television and computers were not part of daily living, and we did not receive information as quickly as we do today. However, as the communication age has exploded with instant communication around the world, many more options and opinions are available to us daily. What are we to do?

More than ever, there is a need for each of us to develop the art of seeking our own psychic intuitive guidance. Of course, I listen to the experts, but with so many conflicting opinions, I have to tune into my psychic intuitive guidance to help me decide which opinion to follow. And it may turn out that I do not follow any of the advice given, but follow another plan of my own. Over the years I have had many experiences, as I am sure many of you have had, that have left me less than confident about immediately following the advice of someone else.

When I was in my twenties, one of the best gynecologists in New York City prescribed treatments for me that are now thought to be inadvisable; but my children might never have been born if I had not followed those treatments. In my thirties, I gave up eating butter and ate margarine, only to find out in my fifties that margarine had been a huge mistake. In my forties and fifties, avocados, egg yolks, and nuts were on the "no-no" list. Now, they are becoming heroes.

In my sixties, I am finally beginning to understand that the answers and the advice are going to keep changing! Ultimately, each one of us is going to have to make decisions on our own. We are simply overloaded with too many choices and opinions. I no longer, as a matter of course, accept what a so-called expert says, because there are too many of them out there giving me conflicting advice.

We are in an age where scientific advances are being made every day. Every time a discovery is made we hear about it. And we also hear about discoveries that contradict every other discovery. Gone are the days when you had a problem and just "did what the doctor or therapist said."

It is only fair to say "Bravo" to all the experts who do the research and give us the advice. While it is true that we are overloaded with information and opinions, the quality of our lives is improving because research is better than it has ever been. While the experts do give us opinions and updates that are conflicting, I would never want research to slow down. However, because the advice keeps changing, it *does* mean that we have to develop the intuitive skills to navigate through this barrage of information.

That does not mean that I am going to make any major decisions without consulting "the experts." I have learned that I have to do the best research I can in order to *evaluate* the opinions I have been given and to decide who is really an expert. Then, having eliminated those opinions not worth listening to, I have to trust my gut instinct as to which of the remaining opinions to follow.

Do not use my advice about the Psychic Intuitive Guidance Process as an excuse for not doing your homework when making an important decision. Anyone who has a health, financial, or other serious problem should consult the experts. But often we receive conflicting opinions, and we have to make our own decisions about which experts' advice to follow. I take the research I have done very seriously, but I also know that with so many conflicting and changing opinions, I have to go deep within and tune into my psychic intuitive guidance and see what feels right!

We're on Decision-Making Overload!

Even when making small decisions, we have so many options. Yesterday, when I walked into the supermarket to buy a jar of peanut butter, I had so many choices: smooth, chunky, or low-fat. There were also many brands of peanut butter to choose from. It is almost overwhelming to walk down the cereal aisle of a large supermarket. You have to know what brand you are looking for or you will get dizzy.

We have a multitude of choices in everything from food items to kinds of toilet paper to clothing. And experts telling us how to do everything. While I am not suggesting that you need to tune in to your intuition each time you choose a brand of peanut butter, we are faced with so many choices and so many opinions that it has become more important than ever that you and I tune into our own psychic intuitive guidance.

Some people become so overwhelmed by the choices available that they want others to decide for them. The person who cannot even order a meal in a restaurant has reached a point of decision-making saturation. Her soul is screaming, "I can't stand to make one more decision today. I am on decision-making overload!"

Peace of Mind Is Yours as You Cope with Change and Make Decisions

It has been said that while we cannot control what happens in life, we can control the manner in which we respond to changes. As you learn to use the tools of the process in this book and CD and begin to tune into your psychic intuitive guidance, you will realize that you always have options. Right now, you may understand that intellectually, but you may not know it on a deep soul level. None of us have to be victims of change. We are spiritual beings with many options available. We can make better moment-to-moment choices and be in a better mood most of the time, if we are willing to listen to our own guidance. Remember:

- Contemplate "all is change."

- Listen to the experts but also consult your psychic intuitive guidance.

- Understand that most of us are on decision-making overload.

It is my hope that as you have read the first three chapters of this book, you have become convinced that you have deep within you the answers that you need to live a better life.

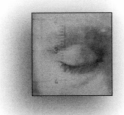

Chapter 4

AN OVERVIEW OF THE PSYCHIC INTUITIVE GUIDANCE PROCESS

Do you have the patience to read all the chapters in part 1 before giving yourself your first intuitive reading, or are you the type that "just can't wait"? If you are so excited that you must try the process *now,* then read this chapter, give yourself an intuitive reading, and *then* read all of the chapters in part 1 before giving yourself more readings. For those of you who have more patience, please read all of the chapters in part 1 before giving yourself an intuitive reading. For those with patience, this chapter serves as an overview of the process.

In the earlier chapters you read about the need to call on your psychic intuitive guidance. Be aware that reading, understanding, and contemplating is one thing, and actually working with the process is another.

Here is how the Psychic Intuitive Guidance Process works:

When you are aware either that you are having a problem or need to make a decision, let your intuition be your guide as you ask a question that frames the problem or decision. Your intuition will lead you to select one of the messages in part 2 of this book that you need to read in this moment. You will select the message through your relationship to the Twelve Energies and the Four States of Being, which you will read about shortly.

As you read the message silently or out loud, listen to the CD track that is listed by number at the top of the message page. After reading and listening, you will notice how you are reacting and what your psychic intuitive guidance is telling you. The message and the music will act as a catalyst for you to delve into your own intuitive wisdom.

How to Give Yourself an Intuitive Reading

First, familiarize yourself with the Twelve Energies.
The Twelve Energies are parts of each one of us that we can call on whenever we need to. What I am calling "energies" some might call archetypes. I prefer to call them energies, as each one has a very different quality and unique vibration. As you contemplate the Twelve Energies, you can call on the part of yourself that you need and you will receive that quality *instantly*.

The Twelve Energies
Full descriptions of the Twelve Energies are given in chapter 5, but they are listed here:

1. The Observer

2. The Soloist

3. The Producer

4. The Voter

5. The Warrior

6. The Nurturer

7. The Seeker

8. The Communicator

9. The Lover

10. The Peacemaker

11. The Devotee

12. The Healer

None of the Twelve Energies is good or bad, right or wrong. For example, one of the Twelve Energies is called "The Observer." This is the part of each one of us that can stand back and observe and witness all that we do. This is a great quality, and sometimes we need to move into it so that we can be more observant of our own behavior, and at another moment we may need to move away from that part of us that observes, as we have been observing *too* much and are becoming overly self-conscious. We call on our psychic intuitive guidance not only to tell us *which* of the Twelve Energies we need to relate to, but *how* we need to relate.

Second, familiarize yourself with the Four States of Being.
It is how we relate to each Energy in the moment that is important. Do we need to move into that Energy or away from it? Do we need to stay still in the essence of that Energy or do we need a new creation of that part of ourselves?

The Four States of Being
Full descriptions of the Four States of Being appear in chapter 6.

They are listed briefly here:

1. Moving Toward

2. Retreating From

3. Birth and Creation

4. Still in the Essence Of

Third, combine an Energy and a State of Being.
Combine one of the Twelve Energies with one of the Four States of Being, which will lead you to the message you need to read in this moment. It's easy.

1. Ask a question about your life.

2. Ask your psychic inner guidance which of the Twelve Energies you need to relate to at this time. Just glance at the list of Twelve Energies on pages 28 and 29 and see which one you feel drawn to.

3. Ask your psychic inner guidance which of the Four States of Being you need to combine with that Energy. Do you need to be moving forward and into this Energy, retreating from this Energy, asking for new birth and the creation of an aspect of this Energy, or do you need to be still in the pure essence of this Energy? Allow your psychic inner guidance to direct you to one of the Four States of Being and then combine that state with the Energy you have chosen. For instance, if you are drawn to the energy called "The Observer," there are Four States of Being that you can choose from to combine with this Energy:

Observer-Moving Toward

Observer-Retreating From

Observer-Birth and Creation

Observer-Still in the Essence Of

4. Once you know the Energy and the State of Being, turn to the list of messages, beginning on page 67, to learn where you can find the message that goes with that Energy-State of Being combination. Then turn to that page and read the written message while listening to the track on the CD that is listed at the top of the page. As you read the message and listen to the music, allow your psychic inner guidance to speak to you and help you to understand how the message you are reading relates to the question that you asked. You will notice that certain words or phrases in the message you are reading will jump out at you. You will also notice that thoughts are coming into your mind that relate to the question you asked.

5. If you like, write down the question each time you ask one and write down the Energy-State of Being combination that you feel guided to explore. Also write down the page number of the message that you are led to. After you have read the message, you may want to write down whatever thoughts you are having as a result of your experience with the message and the music.

Here is a sample form you might like to use each time you give yourself an intuitive reading.

PSYCHIC INTUITIVE GUIDANCE READING FORM

Date: _____

The Question: _____

Describe the situation or mood that the question relates to: _____

Which Energy do I need in this moment? _____

Which of the Four States of Being do I need to combine with that Energy? _____

Number of message: _____

Page number of message: _____

Track on CD: _____

The words in the message that jumped out at me: _____

_____

My reactions after reading the message and listening to the music: _____

Following is a sample reading:

PSYCHIC INTUITIVE GUIDANCE READING FORM

Date: May 17, 2005

The Question: Is it time for me to start looking for a new job?

Describe the situation or mood that the question relates to: I have heard rumors at work lately that there is going to be a downsizing in the company I am working for.

Which Energy do I need in this moment? The Producer

Which of the Four States of Being do I need to combine with that Energy? Moving Toward

Number of message: #9

Page number of message: page 78

Track on CD: #4

The words in the message that jumped out at me: "In this moment I am making a commitment to make a 'to do' list. Then I will decide approximately how long I need to complete each step of the process."

My reactions after reading the message and listening to the music: As I read the message out loud and listened to the motivational music I felt enthusiastic. This experience is helping me face the fact that I may lose my job. I need to start exploring other opportunities so that if I do lose my job, I will already have a good idea of where my next job may be. And who knows, as I do my research, I may find a company I would rather work for even if I don't lose my job. Maybe I will quit. Time will tell. The important thing is that I feel excited about what the possibilities are rather than feeling fear of the future.

Now that you have some understanding of the Twelve Energies and the Four States of Being, in chapters 5 and 6 you will read about the tools in depth.

Ready? Let's move on!

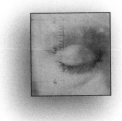

Chapter 5

THE TWELVE ENERGIES

You may rightfully wonder how I came up with the list of the Twelve Energies: the Observer, the Soloist, the Producer, the Voter, the Warrior, the Nurturer, the Seeker, the Communicator, the Lover, the Peacemaker, the Devotee, and the Healer.

I knew that I wanted to develop an intuitive process that would help each of us to tune into our own inner wisdom. I was not interested in developing a divination tool such as tarot cards or rune stones; I wanted a process that would allow us to tune into our inner wisdom without putting any of our power into something else. I am not against such divination tools. I believe that when I use a divination tool, my inner wisdom is causing the stones, the coins, or the sticks to fall in a certain pattern or causing me to pick certain cards. And there are messages of wisdom related to the pattern the stones, sticks, or coins create or the cards that are picked.

I wanted *this* tool, the Psychic Intuitive Guidance Process, to go one step further. I wanted users of the process to ask a question and use our own intuitive guidance to lead us to a message to read. I wanted us all to learn to go into a state of contemplation, and within that state to access our inner wisdom. Therefore I have created tools, the Twelve Energies and the Four States of Being, that ask us to focus our attention in a different way than we would if we were throwing coins or picking cards.

The concept of the Twelve Energies was created as I tuned into my own psychic intuitive guidance. I began to have thoughts about energy and how these different energetic patterns run through each one of us. I could feel the different energetic patterns within myself. I became aware that these patterns express different parts of myself. There is a pattern of energy that fights for things and another pattern of energy that nurtures. The thoughts that I had within periods of deep contemplation led me to the concept of the Twelve Energies. I asked my own intuitive guidance for the names of the Energies, and twelve names came through to me.

When I created what I call the Twelve Energies, I was not thinking at all about archetypes, and it was months later that I realized that what I had done was to bring through a tool similar to the concept of archetypes. The *New American Heritage Dictionary* defines the word *archetype* as "an original model or type after which other similar things are patterned: a prototype. An ideal." I am struck by the words *an original model* and *an ideal.* From my perspective, each of the Twelve Energies *is* an original model of an ideal that is playing itself out energetically within each one of us. It is my spiritual belief that these energetic patterns are parts of us that are connected to the Divine energy of the Creator of All That Is.

There have been many people over the ages who have written and spoken about archetypes: Carl Jung, Joseph Campbell, and Caroline Myss immediately come to mind. This book does not contain a history of the work on archetypes; it does give you a view of the way I have, without planning it, intuitively related to the concept of archetypes as I created the concept of the Twelve Energies.

Our descriptions of the Supreme Being and the ways in which we connect to the Divine are extremely important, as it is by walking our various spiritual paths that we become closer to the Divine and evolve as spiritual beings. The Twelve Energies and the Four States of Being are tools to help you access your inner wisdom, which I believe is ultimately connected to the Divine.

I believe that when we call on these different energetic parts of ourselves, we are calling on an energy that resides within us in *an ideal state*. So if I am calling on the part of myself I call the Energy of the Healer, I am calling specifically for that energetic part of myself. Each energetic pattern operates at the highest level of consciousness and is therefore capable of things the conscious mind is not always capable of. As we call on these ideal parts of ourselves, we are learning and growing. Calling on these parts of ourselves can influence our spiritual evolution positively. As we call on these energetic patterns, they become our *teachers*.

I ask you now to acquire a deep understanding of the tools in this process: to take a deeper look at each of the Twelve Energies and Four States of Being, so that you can internalize the essence of each. Then when you do an intuitive reading, your inner guidance will let you know which Energy and which State of Being you need in this moment.

The Twelve Energies

The Observer
I am able to stand back and witness my life. In this state of consciousness I am my higher self, connected closely with all that is Divine.

We are all part of the Cosmic Consciousness. Each of us is here because we have been given the gift of physical life by the Creator of All That Is. This Supreme Power of Creation has been given many names: God, Higher Power, the Divine, the Beloved, Infinite Spirit, Great Spirit, and many other names through the history of humankind.

When we are born into the physical body we begin the life of the individual. While we travel in an individual physical body, we retain our connection to the Source of All Creation. That aspect of each of us that is still connected to the Source is the part that is able to stand back and observe with detachment everything that happens in our daily lives. While our physical and mental being may experience great swings of emotion, ranging from great joy to great anger, the part that is the Observer, with the use of the spiritual eyes and ears, is able to watch all that happens.

As we draw on the Energy of the Observer, we flow into a state of consciousness that is serene and all knowing. We feel connected to the Source of All Creation.

Music for the Observer is on track 2 of the CD.

The Soloist

I am born alone and I will die alone. My consciousness is
my own, and no other individual is ever able to experience my
perception.

While we are born from the union of our parents and live as human beings with others and walk the spiritual path with others, there is the part of us that is alone. Each one of us is the Soloist, with our own thoughts and perceptions of life. Each of us has our own path to walk and our own responsibilities as we live out our human lives.

We are all soloists. While we live with others and work with others, the actions that each one of us takes are a reflection of each of our individual souls. The Soloist is that part of ourselves that takes responsibility for what we do.

The Soloist needs time alone in order to grow and mature. As we spend time alone, we can hear the echoes of our own thoughts and begin to understand who we are. We talk to ourselves about things and come to understandings.

In the orchestra, the Soloist may be playing music with others. While the violin soloist plays, she may have a conductor guiding her to keep the tempo and guiding her in her expressions of loud and soft playing of the violin, but she is the one playing her violin, and no one else is helping her play it.

Music for the Soloist is on track 3 of the CD.

The Producer

I am the worker, the creator. I take care of my life. I do the tasks that need to be done. I have the energy necessary for carrying out the tasks of my daily life.

From the time we are born we learn how to "do" things. As babies we learn to turn over in the crib, hold our own bottles or baby cups. We learn to crawl and walk, play with toys, and talk. We learn to dress ourselves, make a sandwich, and get ready for school in time.

We grow up learning how to do things and to take responsibility for our lives. We learn to read and write, paint and draw. Each day, each year, we take on increasing responsibility for our own lives.

We have physical, mental, and emotional energy that takes us through the day. Most of us do not sit in a state of meditation all day, and need to get up and get going.

There is a part of each one of us that is the Producer. This part of us produces and carries out all the tasks of the day. This is the part of us that creates projects, makes outlines, and carries out the project. This is the part of us that goes to the hardware store, buys the nails, and fixes the house. This is the part that buys the groceries and makes the dinner. This energy within goes to work, creates projects, attends meetings, and gets things done.

The Producer Within is energetic, task oriented, organized. While each of us plays the role of the Producer in different styles with various modes of organization and energy, we all have tasks to carry out, so the Producer Within plays a very important part in daily life.

Music of the Producer is on track 4 of the CD.

The Voter

I am loyal to others and myself. I make choices each day about who to befriend and who to stand back from. As I make choices, I cast my vote. I am decisive and able to choose.

As we grow up we learn to make choices. Our first choices are about when we want to eat and when we don't. Babies know quite easily when they want milk and when they are finished. Small children know what foods they want to eat and which foods they don't want to eat.

As we get older there are many more choices to make, and many more voices trying to tell us what choices to make. Our parents tell us, our siblings tell us, our teachers tell us, our friends tell us, and the characters on television and in books try to persuade us about what we should and should not do. Making choices becomes confusing, to the point where many of us do not know what we want. And then when we make a choice, we still have questions such as "Is this what I really wanted, or am I making this choice because someone else wants me to make this choice?"

The Voter is that part within each one of us that is able to *know* what it wants and can make a choice with integrity. When we have many options and many people telling us what to do, it is the Voter Within that we call on to come to our aid and make a decision.

The Voter is able to cope with confusion, lots of choices, and then make a decision. The Voter knows that everyone will not agree and that the choice made may be popular or unpopular. But the Voter holds its head high and says, "This is my choice, like it or not." The Energy of the Voter makes it possible to work within the family and the larger community and hold on to one's opinions.

The Voter Within will help you choose your work, your mate, your friends, and what you spend your time doing. And when you are going in a direction with choices that no longer serve you, it is the Voter Within that will be there for you once again to make a new choice and start you off in a new direction.

Music of the Voter is on track 5 of the CD.

The Warrior
I am the survivor. I am the fighter. I rise to the occasion and take on the challenges of my existence.

As we grow up, there comes a time when we begin to fight many of our own battles. For some of us, this time comes all too soon when we are the children of parents who are not able to protect us. Some of us have parents who are able to monitor with wisdom how much protection we need and who also have the ability to know when we need to start fighting our own battles. Ideally, all of us grow up and become independent and fight our own battles.

Those of us who want to hang on to the protection of others choose friends or mates who protect us. Or we choose ways of living in which we give up our authority and let others make our decisions and protect us.

The fullest life that is lived with the deepest integrity is that life in which the Warrior is able to live out its missions and destinies. The Warrior will not always choose the easiest route, but the path chosen will be the path of integrity.

When you need to survive difficult situations, it is the Warrior Within that needs to be called into action. When you are experiencing loss and it seems that life will never again be worthwhile, it is the Warrior who needs to spring into action, bringing you the energy of survival.

The Warrior takes steady steps, always alert as to what the next action needs to be. The Warrior does not throw its fists around, out of control. The Warrior knows instinctively what to do. The Warrior is the martial artist using the energy at hand perfectly and with great precision.

Music of the Warrior is on track 6 of the CD.

The Nurturer

I am a friend to myself. I am a friend to others. I take care of my loved ones and myself. I take care of my world. I am the steward.

We all have a responsibility to take care of others and ourselves. And as time goes on, we are becoming more aware of the responsibilities that we have forgotten and must reclaim for taking care of and nurturing our home: the planet Earth.

Humankind used to be involved with its small village, then its larger city or town. And as the history of humankind has progressed and developed faster and more complicated modes of travel and communication, humankind's view is no longer of the small village, but of the whole planet Earth and the universe of which our planet is but a tiny speck.

The Nurturer Within knows that everything that exists needs care. The physical body is not able to take care of itself without the cooperation of the spirit that is living within it. Healthy meals need to be prepared, teeth need to be brushed, visits to the doctor and dentist need to be made. The Nurturer also knows that one's caring also extends to friends and loved ones. We need to help each other along the path of life. Friends and lovers need to be held and listened to. Our children, elderly parents, and the sick and physically and/or mentally challenged need to be taken care of and nurtured.

The Nurturer Within can see that our planet needs attention and care. We need to use the resources of the Earth in a responsible manner, and we need to reach out to those around the planet that are starving and without medical help and supplies.

The Nurturer is willing to give up some of what it has to give to others. When you are faced with situations where you want to be giving to yourself or those around you, it is the Nurturer Within that you must call to. This loving energetic vibration will surround you and yours with love and attention.

Music of the Nurturer is on track 7 of the CD.

The Seeker

I am the spiritual seeker, the adventurer. I allow myself to flow into the mystery of all life and all eternity.

Within each one of us lives the Seeker of spiritual knowledge. The Creator of All That Is is always a step ahead of the Seeker, so the Seeker is always learning more and evolving spiritually. The Seeker Within takes one on the spiritual path of knowledge and wisdom, one step at a time.

The Energy of the Seeker will never allow you to become complacent and declare that you have "arrived." It is the Seeker Within who will argue with you if you start thinking that you "know it all!" And in fact, when others in your life make such egocentric declarations, it is the Seeker Within who will prompt you to take a step back from people like that. The Seeker Within knows that all knowledge cannot be expressed and declared by any individual. The Seeker Within will never become stagnant and knows that the mystery of life is always unfolding.

When you are feeling the need to take another step on the spiritual path, call on the part of you that is the Seeker. Sometimes we become so involved in the tasks of daily life that the vibrations of the spiritual path seem like a distant memory. But the energy of the spiritual path is only a breath away, if you just focus on and call the Seeker Within.

Music of the Seeker is on track 8 of the CD.

The Communicator

I talk to others. I talk to myself. I express my ideas, my feelings, and my creativity.

There is so much inside of each one of us that wants to be expressed. We want to share our thoughts and feelings with others in our lives. Sometimes the thoughts we want to communicate are personal feelings, and at other times we just want to communicate something as simple as "I want to meet for lunch at twelve o'clock."

The Communicator is that part of each of us that shares with the world. Sometimes the communications are internal, in that we are talking to ourselves: making decisions, going back and forth trying to decide. Sometimes we are admitting to ourselves how we feel about a situation or person.

At other times, our communications are external, as we write letters, make phone calls, or speak at meetings. We communicate as we relate to everyone with whom we come into contact, including our pets.

It is the Communicator Within that is working when we write books, compose music, and create works of art. Our messages are delivered in paintings, plays, and all forms of communication.

The Communicator has a difficult job to do, as those to whom we express ourselves do not always accept our communications. Sometimes the Communicator has the best intentions as we express ourselves to other people, and those who receive the messages do not always react in the manner we would have liked. Call on the Communicator Within to help you communicate in the best possible way. The Communicator has more wisdom on a subconscious and higher level than your conscious everyday mind. The Communicator Within will help you to take a deep breath and weigh your words carefully. You will be less likely to say things that you wish you could take back.

The Communicator will help you to put yourself in another's shoes before speaking. You will be less likely to make critical statements to others without first understanding how the others are feeling.

Music of the Communicator is on track 9 of the CD.

The Lover

I am in love with life's every moment. Each instant I choose love. I love myself, I love my neighbor. I love the trees and the flowers, the animals. I love all that is, and every instant inside and outside of time.

You have within you the choice every day to love life or to dislike life. Every second brings you an opportunity to get the best out of life. Getting the best does not always mean feeling happy every second. Getting the best involves taking the positive out of every second, rather than choosing the negative.

The Lover is that part of us that is able to choose joy. Sometimes joy is the painful learning that you experience when you learn something valuable even though you are in a difficult situation. Sometimes joy is knowing that you are able to cope with a difficult situation.

The Lover has spiritual eyes and ears that see the beauty in all that exists. Every sunset is a gift, every raindrop is a gift. Every breath of life is pure joy to the Lover Within.

When you are in rhythm with the Lover Within, all of your relationships will be more compassionate. Your desire to compete with others in a destructive manner will be transformed into knowing that there is plenty of all that we need in life. We do not have to take from each other in ways that are not caring.

The Lover Within knows that to be a friend is to have a friend. As you get into the rhythm of the vibrations of the Lover, you will have a smile and an energetic embrace for all with whom you come into contact. This does not mean that you will hug everyone you see, but your energetic vibrations will extend from your physical body, and those who come into contact with you will feel the warmth of your joy for life and your love.

Call on the Lover when you need to be more in touch with your innate ability to enjoy life and experience the best from every situation, every person, and every moment of your life.

Music of the Lover is on track 10 of the CD.

The Peacemaker

I make peace with myself. I make peace with others. When I leave my physical body for the eternal world, I will be at peace with All.

You are love. You are at peace within yourself and with all whom you come into contact with. When this is not true, there is a tension within, knowing that your being is in conflict with others. The Peacemaker is dedicated to an awareness of all situations that need to be resolved. You do not want to leave this world still in conflict with those you love.

The Peacemaker Within knows that it is important to make peace with those with whom we have had conflicts, even though talking things over and making compromises with people can be difficult and emotionally painful.

The Peacemaker Within is not interested in sweeping controversial issues under the rug where anger can grow and create emotional destruction. The Peacemaker vibrations within you are ready to face problems and resolve issues.

Sometimes the Peacemaker has been misunderstood and thought of as an energy that always gives in and will do anything to avoid an argument. But the true Peacemaker will never agree to anything just to avoid a confrontation. When you are influenced by the vibrations of the Peacemaker Within you will never agree to things that will leave you angry inside. You will take the time and expend the emotional energy to come to an agreement with another person that you can truly live with. Will you totally have your way? Perhaps not! But the Peacemaker will help you negotiate with others and come to compromises that you feel proud of.

The Peacemaker will also help you be at peace with yourself, which as we know, is not always easy. Call on the Peacemaker whenever you need peace of mind. The Peacemaker will know in all wisdom what needs resolving and will guide you.

Music of the Peacemaker is on track 11 of the CD.

The Devotee

I am sincere and disciplined in my devotion. I make time for my devotional practice.

There is a part of each of us that yearns. We long to be in touch with that part that is the Devotee. People express devotion in many different ways. Some of you are devoted to making quilts, painting pictures, or growing vegetable gardens. Some of you are devoted to working long hours or raising children. Devotion is commitment in action.

The Devotee Within longs for spiritual devotion. When you make a spiritual choice and choose a spiritual path, the Devotee Within is able to play its role and blossom. When the vibrations of the Devotee influence you, you feel sure of your spiritual direction:

you spend the time in devotion and allow yourself the benefits of the spiritual path you have chosen.

The Energy of the Devotee is peaceful and sure of itself. Allow yourself to experience the Devotee Within even if you are not yet ready to choose a spiritual path. The vibrations can bring calm and peace to your soul and prepare you for the choice you will make when you are ready.

The Devotee is not interested in changing its mind every other day. The true Energy of the Devotee does not change spiritual paths every day like one changes clothes. The Devotee Within is there to be experienced when you are ready to devote yourself to a spiritual path that has been chosen with wisdom.

Call on the Devotee Within when you want to experience the vibrations of devotion to either calm your soul as you choose a spiritual path or to be your friend as you continue your devotional practices on a chosen path.

Music for the Devotee is on track 12 of the CD.

The Healer

As I receive the healing energy from the Creator of All That Is,
I receive and pass on the vibrations of healing energy.

You cannot heal. You cannot heal yourself or anyone else. What you *can* do is to call to the Healer within your being that is connected to the Creator of All That Is. You can call to that part of yourself that is able to channel the healing energies of the universe.

Every moment of life offers you a chance to heal. As your mind buzzes with conflicts, you can choose healing. You can call to the Healer Within that knows that all conflicts are only perceptions of the mind. All is love, and all is healing.

The Healer Within knows that each one of us is connected to the Divine Creator. While each one of us may have a different name for the Supreme Power of Creation, we are nevertheless all connected and part of the same essence. There is no fear when you are connected and influenced by the Healer Within.

Call on the Healer when you are feeling disturbed by physical, emotional, and spiritual vibrations. The Healer Within brings a peace that words can never describe. Call on the Healer when you want to send healing thoughts and vibrations to other people and situations in the world and greater universe.

The Healer Within is ultimate peace and understanding. The Healer knows all, contains all wisdom. The Healer Within is your best friend, your passion, and your connection with the Creator of All That Is.

Music of the Healer is on track 13 of the CD.

As you become familiar with the Twelve Energies, let them become part of you in a very creative and fluid manner. Allow yourself to feel as if each Energy has its own special vibration that can wash over and through your entire being. If you like, see each Energy as a beautiful mist that can penetrate your physical, emotional, and spiritual bodies.

Which Energy Do I Need?

The Twelve Energies are parts of ourselves that we can call on simply by contemplating the quality of the Energy. Read and reread the descriptions of the Twelve Energies, so that when you want to give yourself an intuitive reading and you ask, "Which of the Twelve Energies do I need in this moment?" your intuitive inner voice will be so familiar with the energies that the one you need will instantly be revealed to you. You may hear the name of the Energy in your mind, or the thought of a particular Energy will suddenly flow into your consciousness.

Not only can you call on any of the Twelve Energies when you want to give yourself an intuitive reading, but you can call on them at any time during the day or night when you have a need. You do not always have to give yourself a reading. There may be times when you are feeling discombobulated and you simply need to get in touch with a part of yourself that will help you to feel in balance once again. And there will be times when you do not have the time or are not in a situation where you are able to give yourself an intuitive reading. You can still call on any of the Twelve Energies.

In chapter 6, you will read about the Four States of Being. This tool will help you intuitively understand how you need to relate to a specific Energy. Sometimes you may need to be moving into an Energy, while at other times you need to be retreating from that Energy. Go on now to the next chapter, and learn how the Twelve Energies and the Four States of Being relate to each other.

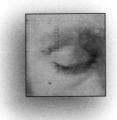

Chapter 6

THE FOUR STATES OF BEING

Life is change, and the way we relate to every aspect of our lives will always be changing. Therefore, we cannot find a solution that will always work, because the nature of the problem at hand will always be changing.

As you use the Psychic Intuitive Guidance Process, you will first listen to your inner guidance to select which of the Twelve Energies you need in the moment. But knowing the Energy you need is not enough. You still must discern what relationship you need to this Energy. It may be that you need to move *forward and into* the Energy, or it may be that you need to *retreat or step back from* it. Another possibility is that you need a *new birth and creation* of an aspect of the Energy. A fourth possibility is that you may need to *be still and immerse yourself* in it.

Let me caution you against trying to figure out logically what Energy and State of Being you need. This is not a logical process. There is a certain amount of mystery involved as you delve into your intuitive process. So if at this moment, your mind does not understand everything perfectly, be assured that your soul may.

Continue reading, and it will all become evident as to how the process works.

Before you are ready to choose a State of Being, you need to become familiar with your choices, just as you became familiar with your choices of Energy in the previous chapter.

The best way to become familiar with the Four States of Being is to listen to track 1 on the CD while reading the text of the meditation in this chapter. This twenty-minute meditation will take you through the Four States of Being. The words spoken in this meditation came through to me when I was in a deep state of reflection and inspiration. I spoke the words that I heard spontaneously, from my own psychic intuitive guidance, as I recorded the spoken words over the music. Enjoy the experience as you listen to the guided meditation on the CD.

Four States of Being Meditation (Track 1 on CD)

Introduction

In this meditation I explore and experience Four States of Being.

I experience these four states so that I can call on each one when it is needed.

Life is change and every moment brings change.

All is vibration.

As I live my life I move through Four States of Being.

Sometimes I am moving forward,

Sometimes retreating,

There are times when I am enveloped with the birth of new aspects of my being.

There are times when I am still feeling the pure essence of what is in the moment.

Moving Forward, Moving Into

In this moment I move forward,
I move toward,
I move into,
I become more a part of,
I am carried in this moment by the vibration of stepping
into and moving forward.
I move at a steady pace
Slowly
Slowly
Moving forward
Moving into

Contemplate this State of Being for several minutes as you listen to the rest of the music of the State of Being called "Moving Toward."

Retreating From, Moving Back

Life is change.
Every moment brings change.
All is vibration.
As I live my life I move through Four States of Being,
Sometimes moving forward
Sometimes retreating
There are times when I am enveloped with the birth of
new aspects of my being
And times when I am still feeling the pure essence of what
is in the moment.
In this moment I am retreating,
I am moving away from.
There is a knowing within that says, Back up
Stay clear

Retreat now.
In this moment I am stepping back
I am distancing myself
I do not need to run
I do not need to flee
I will not create any drama
I step back slowly
I need to stand on the sideline, not in the center
I am stepping back leaving others in the center.
I step back slowly
I step back peacefully
I step back with grace on my side.

Contemplate "Retreating From" as you listen to the rest of the music that reflects this State of Being.

New Birth, New Creation

Life is change, every moment brings change.
In this moment there is creation
There is passion
There is fire
There is birth
A new idea
A new creation
A new love
A new passion.
Energies stir within my soul
And new aspects are born in this moment.
All is excitement
All is wonderment
I am in awe as I experience new creation
New birth.

Contemplate this State of Being for several minutes as you listen to the rest of the music of the State of Being called "Birth and Creation."

Still in the Pure Essence

Life is change
And sometimes it feels like there is no movement.
It is as if time has stopped.
I enter a new dimension.
In this moment I am still.
I am not moving forward
I am not retreating
I am not experiencing passion or new birth.
I am still
I am quiet
I am immersed in the pure essence of what is.
This is the moment when time stops.
I experience the glory of the nature of what is in this
*   moment.*
I experience the pure essence of my being
Every aspect of my soul.
I experience all that has been
All that is now and will ever be
Only the essence
Only the essence
Only the essence.

Contemplate "Still in the Essence of" as you listen to the rest of the music that reflects this State of Being.

Conclusion

In this meditation I have experienced Four States of Being.
I have moved forward
I have retreated
I have experienced new birth

And I have become still and immersed in pure essence.
I can call on each of these States of Being as the moment
  requires.
I am flexible
I am strong
I am in touch with the aspects of my soul
I can move in many directions and in many ways
I can handle any situation that is presented to me.
I am grateful to the Creator of All That Is.
I am at peace.

After listening to the meditation of the Four States of Being, turn off the CD and sit in silence for a few minutes. Experiencing silence after listening to music is one of the most wonderful experiences I have ever had. The quality of the silence is very much affected by the experience you have just had. If you listen to this meditation many times, each time will be a new experience, and the silence that follows will feel different as a result.

Allow your psychic intuitive guidance to speak to you during the time you listen to the meditation and during the silence afterward. What has your inner voice told you about the Four States of Being and how you relate to each one? Do some of the states come naturally to you, while others feel more foreign? Jot down your thoughts in a notebook.

Now that you are familiar with the Twelve Energies and the Four States of Being, you are ready to learn, in chapter 7, about the Energy-State of Being Combinations, and how to find the message that relates to the combination you have chosen.

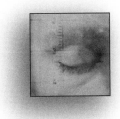

THE ENERGY-STATE OF BEING COMBINATION

Just for practice, let's choose one of the Twelve Energies you have just read about and look at it as we combine it with each of the Four States of Being.

Let's use the example of the Nurturer. There are four possible Energy-State of Being combinations:

1. Nurturer-Moving Toward

2. Nurturer-Retreating From

3. Nurturer-Birth and Creation

4. Nurturer-Still in the Pure Essence Of

Moving Toward

If you are *moving toward* the Energy of the Nurturer, you will become more involved in this Energy. Moving toward the Energy of the Nurturer might be useful when you need to take care of someone, including yourself.

Retreating From

If you need to be *retreating from* the Energy of the Nurturer, you will be moving away from and becoming less involved in this Energy. This might be useful when you have been taking care of someone and need a break.

Birth and Creation

If you need *birth and creation* of the Energy of the Nurturer, there is a reason why. Perhaps you are in a situation where you must care for someone and you are exhausted. You need not only rest, but the birth of a whole new Energy. Or perhaps you have never been much of a nurturer and you need the creation of the kind of Energy that will enhance your ability to take care of yourself and others.

Still in the Pure Essence Of

In this case, you do not need to be moving toward or retreating from the Energy of the Nurturer. Perhaps you need to *be still and experience the pure essence* of the Nurturer.

When you give yourself an intuitive reading, you will ask your intuition which Energy and State of Being you need. Then you will turn to part 2, entitled "The Messages." On pages 67–69 is a list of all the possible Energy-State of Being Combinations and the page number of the message that relates to each combination.

A Caution

The previous example is a logical look at how each of the Four States of Being *might* relate to the Energy of the Nurturer. Why do I use the word *might*? Logic is not ultimately what the Psychic Intuitive Guidance Process is all about. When you ask a question about your life and then allow your intuition to lead you to an Energy and a State of Being, what happens within your mind as you read the selected message and listen to the music will be a unique experience. While I can provide examples of what *might* happen, I cannot know what *will* happen for you each time you give yourself an intuitive reading using the Psychic Intuitive Guidance Process. That is the beauty of the process. It becomes yours, not mine. All I can do is teach you the process and supply you with the tools. The results as you use the process are all yours and cannot be predetermined.

What you experience as you work with the Twelve Energies and the Four States of Being will be your unique experience. Once you have given yourself a number of intuitive readings, compare your experiences with the experiences of others that are described in part 3 of this book.

If you can't wait to give yourself an intuitive reading, go back and read chapter 4, "An Overview of the Psychic Intuitive Guidance Process." Then you can immediately give yourself a reading, and read chapter 8 later. But for those of you who like the slow and steady approach, let's move on now to chapter 8, and read about the music and meditations that are on the CD.

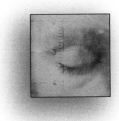

USING THE MUSIC

The music on the CD is an extremely important ingredient of the Psychic Intuitive Guidance Process. Music has always been part of the experience of human beings, particularly in spiritual pathways of all kinds. When I think about my own early childhood religious education, music was always part of the experience. And as an adult, music has been an integral part of my spiritual exploration.

The Psychic Intuitive Guidance CD

I have created a CD for you to listen to as you read the messages in this book so that you will have a "multimedia" experience. You will be affected not only by the words you are reading, but also by the music playing in the background as you read the words.

The Four States of Being Meditation: Track 1
Listen to this twenty-minute meditation when you want to remind yourself that life is continuously changing and that you need to

respond to each situation in a manner that is best in the moment. There will be times in life when you need to move forward and into a situation or forward and into a particular Energy. There will also be times when you need to retreat from a situation or from the strength of an Energy. There will be times that you need to ask the universe for the birth and creation of new Energy, and times you need to be still in the essence of a situation or of an Energy.

As you listen to this meditation, you will experience the vibrations of these four different states through the music. While I do guide the meditation with words, they are brief. The words at the beginning of each section of the meditation serve only to announce which State of Being the music is expressing.

As you listen to the meditation of the Four States of Being, allow yourself to internalize the essence of each State of Being, so that you can call on that state anytime you need it.

Music of the Twelve Energies

Each of the Twelve Energies has its own vibration and therefore its own musical piece on the CD. This music has been composed to stimulate the vibrations of each Energy: the music of the Producer has been composed to activate the vibrations of productivity within you as listen to it, while the music of the Nurturer has an entirely different sound that has been composed to activate the vibrations of the nurturing qualities within you.

Playing the CD

When you have intuitively chosen an Energy and a State of Being combination, adjust the volume of the music accordingly:

- For instance, if you have chosen the combination The Devotee-Moving Forward, play the music of the Devotee at a normal and comfortable listening volume. As you listen to the music, imagine that you are moving into this Energy and it is increasing its vibration at this time.

- However, if you have chosen the combination The Devotee-Retreating From, then play the music of the Devotee at a low volume that is almost hard to hear. In this case, you want the Energy of the Devotee to be in the background of your life. As you listen to the music, imagine that this Energy is diminishing for the present moment.

- If you have chosen the combination The Devotee-Birth and Creation, play the music of the Devotee louder than you would normally play it. In this instance, you are asking for a new birth of the Energy of the Devotee and you want the vibrations of the music to penetrate. Open your heart and soul to the vibrations of the music and feel revitalized.

- If you have chosen The Devotee-Still in the Essence Of, play the music at a normal and comfortable volume. Sit back and relax into the Energy of the music. Absorb the essence of the music.

Let the music act as a catalyst. Use the music to stimulate the Energies and States of Being that you need at a particular time so that you can make more effective decisions and be in a better mood as you cope with change.

As you become familiar with the music of the Twelve Energies and the Four States of Being, memories of these musical pieces will play in your mind as you need them. For instance, if you are feeling exhausted but still have a lot of work to do, you may suddenly start hearing the music of the Producer playing in your mind. Your intuitive guidance has a way of giving you exactly what you need when you need it. All you have to do is to be open to your inner wisdom. Listen to the CD often, so that the music becomes part of your subconscious.

It is not necessary that you like each piece of music. This music has been composed to stimulate various energies. You may like some of the pieces, and you may dislike other pieces. It makes no difference in the Psychic Intuitive Guidance Process. For instance, the music of the Producer can stimulate the Energy of productivity. If the music does its job, it makes no difference whether you like it or not. And you may find that the piece that is your favorite this week is not next week, and the piece you used to dislike has become your favorite.

Listening to the Music
While Reading the Message

Each time you read a message, listen to the music that goes with that message. You will find that your experience is totally different than if you read the message without listening to the music. First of all, music has a way of distracting us from our thoughts. If you listen to the music while reading the message, there is a much better chance that thoughts such as "What shall I cook for dinner?" will not be running in the back of your mind. The music will fill up your mental space, and there will only be room for you to be conscious of the music and the message you are reading. This will give you a deeper experience of the reactions that you have to the message you are reading.

You know what you need in each moment, and the music and the messages are tools to help you access answers from your inner wisdom. Use these tools together often.

PART 2

The Messages

THE MESSAGES

Following is a list of all the messages and their page numbers. By this time, you will have chosen one of the Twelve Energies and one of the Four States of Being. Look for the combination that you have chosen. You will find the page number for that combination's message next to the title of the combination.

Messages and Page Numbers

Message 1: The Observer-Moving Toward, page 70

Message 2: The Observer-Retreating From, page 71

Message 3: The Observer-Birth and Creation, page 72

Message 4: The Observer-Still in the Essence Of, page 73

Message 5: The Soloist-Moving Toward, page 74

Message 6: The Soloist-Retreating From, page 75

Message 7: The Soloist-Birth and Creation, page 76

Message 8: The Soloist-Still in the Essence Of, page 77

Message 9: The Producer-Moving Toward, page 78

Message I

The Observer-Moving Toward

Listen to track 2 on the CD while reading message silently or out loud. Play music at normal volume while reading the message.

I am taking myself much too seriously. When I am with those I love, I find that I am easily frustrated and get agitated easily. Sometimes I express this agitation, and sometimes I let it bubble inside, making those around me extremely uncomfortable.

At this time, I have lost the ability to practice detachment. I have lost the ability to observe myself without emotion. Instead I am reacting quickly and with great passion to every little thing that happens in my daily life. I feel that I am prone to quick decisions, sudden anger, frequent tears, and confusion.

In this moment, I need to step back from so much emotional involvement and move toward cultivating the role of the Observer in my life. Right now I need to call that part of myself which is the "witness" and ask that this part of me play a greater role in my everyday life.

As I listen to the music of the Observer, I am able to float in the various dimensions of my being. As I allow myself to get past my own thoughts, I begin to flow into the state of consciousness that I call "My Observer, my witness."

In this moment, I ask the Creator of All That Is to be with me as I connect with the Observer.

Message 2

The Observer-Retreating From

Listen to Track 2 on the CD while reading message silently or out loud. Play at a soft volume, as this is an energy you are retreating from and want to be background music in your life at this time.

I am watching myself too closely, observing everything that I do in the hopes of making better decisions. I have become obsessed with self-observation. While in this state of obsession, I do avoid giving in to the strong emotions that take over my being when I am not observing myself. However, during this time of constantly watching myself, I am missing the joys of living that come from being emotionally involved with life.

I am missing the sudden impulse to hug a friend, take a day off work, and go walking in the countryside. I am too busy watching myself.

In this moment, I need to stop watching myself so much. I am misusing the concept of the Observer and going to extremes. I am being overly critical of myself, and this is not doing me any good at all.

As I listen to the music of the Observer, I draw back from that part of myself until a time when I can use that Energy properly and be a true witness and observer, not the self-conscious critic I have been lately.

Message 3

The Observer-Birth and Creation

Listen to track 2 on the CD while reading message silently or out loud. Play the music louder than usual to allow the vibrations of new creation to be in the foreground of your life.

In this moment, I know that the Creator of All That Is brings a new creation of the Observer. I can feel the essence of this quality as it weaves its gentle way into my heart and soul.

While I have been able to practice detachment in my life, allowing myself to stand back and observe myself, in this moment there is a new creation of this quality within me. I know that I am ready to take the next step in my ability to observe myself and be honest with myself. So I am ready to receive a new birth and creation of the Energy of the Observer.

I trust the Creator of All That Is to know when I need a new vibration of the Observer.

I am in wonder and awe as I listen to the music of the Observer. This music allows my mind to stop thinking and to float into the detachment that is so needed in my life. As I listen to the music of the Observer, my body relaxes, making it possible for me to let go of all the busy thoughts that play in my mind. I now let the music carry me into the states of consciousness where I may meet the witness, the Observer of my life.

I give grateful thanks for this new Energy of the Observer that pours within.

Message 4

The Observer-Still in the Essence Of

Listen to track 2 on the CD while reading message silently or out loud. Play at a normal volume.

My life flows smoothly when I am able to take myself less seriously. When I take myself too seriously I am out of balance. In this moment, I am appreciating and experiencing the essence of the Observer. As I contemplate this essence, there is nothing I have to do in this moment. I do not need to observe or witness anything. I am free to immerse myself in the Energy of the Observer so that I become so familiar with this Energy that I can call it to me any time, anywhere, as I need it.

I know the great value of detachment, the ability to step outside one's self and observe what is going on without emotion. I know how important it is to witness my actions, thoughts, and emotions. The Observer is not committed to any decisions, strong emotions, or judgments. The Observer Within watches what is happening and then does nothing but watch.

The Observer, my good friend, never passes judgment, but is present in a loving, supportive way. The Observer says, "This is what is happening. You see yourself in the moment as you truly are."

Is the Observer God's way of helping me to be able to understand what is really happening in my life? If so, then God is demonstrating that I truly have free will and must take responsibility for my life. Because in these moments when the witness is showing me the reality of a moment, there are no instructions that come along with the pictures of reality that I am seeing. I am looking in a special kind of mirror that shows only what is happening at the moment.

Message 5

The Soloist-Moving Toward

Listen to track 3 on the CD while reading message silently or out loud. Play at a normal volume.

I am finding it difficult to spend time with myself. I find myself running around in a circle of activity. While it is nice to be so involved in life with others, I am not finding the solitude that I need.

In this moment, I ask the Creator of All That Is to hear my need and to support me in my search for solitude.

Sometimes all it takes is to let myself know that I need time alone. Once I am in touch with my own need, then I must take a stand with those who do not appreciate my need for solitude.

I must not compare myself to others. There may be those who do not need the solitude that I need at this time. I am on my own journey. I have my own path to follow in this life. Part of that path is time alone.

As I listen to the music of the Soloist I am drawn to the sounds and harmonies that play within. I know that when I spend time alone I will not be lonely, as there will be many things that I will experience within myself. In fact, as I spend time with myself, I will be amazed at the multitudes of experience available to me. I need to be alone to have these experiences. I need to be totally free of the influence of others in order to experience what is truly mine.

As I listen to the voices of my soul, there is harmony created that weaves a pattern of mystical integrity.

As I listen to the music, I am drawn toward spending more time alone.

Message 6

The Soloist-Retreating From

Listen to track 3 on the CD while reading message silently or out loud. Play at a soft volume, as this is an energy you are retreating from and want to be background music in your life at this time.

Hey, it's been great being alone, but I need to get out of here, out of myself. Enough already!

I have learned a great deal being alone, but my time alone has been taking up too much of my life. In this moment, I need to change gears and go in another direction. I need to be with people.

In this moment, I realize that life is about balance, and my life is out of balance.

Balance is a peculiar fellow. Balance never seems to get it quite right, always tipping too far one way or another. But Balance is my best friend, and I will work with Balance in order to find what I need at any given moment. Balance is never really wrong, just a bit "out of balance."

As I listen to the music of the Soloist, I let this Energy fade into the background of my life for awhile. I look forward to the enjoyment of being with people. I will again return to visit the Soloist in another moment, when it is truly the Soloist that I need.

As I listen to the music, I have fantasies of things I would like to do and places I would like to go, with other people!

Message 7

The Soloist-Birth and Creation

Listen to track 3 on the CD while reading message silently or out loud. Play the music louder than usual to allow the vibrations of new creation to be in the foreground of your life.

New comfort is needed. I need to be more comfortable being alone. I am ready. I now take another step in my path of solitude.

In this moment, I ask the Creator of All That Is to create a new energy for the part of me that is the Soloist. I pray that I may become more comfortable being alone. I pray that I may become more accepting of myself. It is my desire to stop running away from myself so that I will be more willing to create time in my life to be alone.

Being alone can sometimes produce fear and anxiety. Being alone can sometimes make me feel like I am missing out on life. But without time alone, I become overwhelmed with the energy of other people.

I often feel the need for others around me but then become overwhelmed with so many things going on at the same time: too many people, too many problems, too many opinions.

Stop turning from mirrors, my soul calls to me. Love yourself as you are. "It is only in being with yourself that you can truly find your heart's desire."

As I listen to the music of the Soloist, I feel new vibrations penetrating my being: vibrations of self-acceptance and ease of being with myself. In this moment, I know that as I spend more time alone I will become closer to my own being. I will become my own best friend.

I listen to the music and let go of all tension. I accept a new creation of the Soloist Within. The voices of my soul weave the harmony of new creation.

Message 8

The Soloist-Still in the Essence Of

Listen to track 3 on the CD while reading message silently or out loud. Play the music at a normal volume.

Sometimes I need to be alone in the stillness of my own vibrations. I need to listen to the sounds of my soul. I need to get away from all the other messages I receive from those in my daily life. It is hard to hear the messages that my soul brings to me when there are messages coming from so many other people, from so many other directions.

In this moment, I need to appreciate and bask in the essence of the part of me that is the Soloist. In the quiet of my own energy field, I can relax and let go. I can listen to the voice of my own soul as it echoes throughout my being. I am in touch with what really matters to me.

As I listen to the music of the Soloist, I hear the harmonic vibrations of my soul. The sound plays within me, searching and inventing that which is really important to my journey. The sounds are sometimes dissonant and not what I am expecting. As I open my heart and soul to the sounds of my own creativity, I am guided to vibrations and paths of knowledge I might not have experienced had I not taken this time to be alone. I allow the mystical harmonies of the voices of my soul to take me into new dimensions. I hear more than one voice singing within me, each playing its part in my heart.

Message 9

The Producer-Moving Toward

Listen to track 4 on the CD while reading message silently or out loud. Play the music at normal volume.

There are so many things I would like to do. I have to admit that I think of lots of great ideas, but I am finding it hard to carry through. I have been talking about several projects, and I notice that I am not taking any actions.

In this moment, I move toward the Energy Within that is The Producer.

I get excited and love sharing my ideas with my friends. My friends get excited also. I have to admit that I like the approval that I get as I talk about my ideas, and I leave these conversations feeling terrific. But then I realize I am only talking about my ideas, and I am not carrying through.

In this moment I am making a commitment to write down some plans. I will choose one project and make a "to do" list. Then I will decide approximately how long I need to complete each step of the project.

As I listen to the music of the Producer, I feel energy pouring into my being. I am becoming energized to take action. I visualize myself working hard toward my goals.

Message 10

The Producer-Retreating From

Listen to track 4 on the CD while reading message silently or out loud. Play at a soft volume, as this is an energy you are retreating from and want to be background music in your life at this time.

Let me *out* of here.

My mind is spinning with all the work I have been doing. I can't think about anything else. The people in my life are starting to give up on me.

There was a time when I understood why I worked. I wanted to earn a living, pay my bills, and make a contribution to the world. I did not care if I made a lot of money. I wanted a good life.

My life is out of control. My work has become the totality of my life. I am out of balance. I don't know how to get off the treadmill that I am on. Every time I try to jump off this merry-go-round, the phone rings and I am back into another work issue.

I pray that I may find a way to slow down and get in contact with my old self again. I miss that part of me that found time to take walks in the park, say hello to people in the grocery store, and call my elderly relatives on the weekend.

I ask the Creator to help me find my way back to sanity. I want a balanced life once again.

As I listen to the music of the Producer, I let go of the pounding and pushing I am doing to achieve. Everything has its time and place, and in this moment, I need to let go of working so hard. As I listen to the music of the Producer, I turn down the volume until I hear nothing but silence around me.

Message 11

The Producer-Birth and Creation

Listen to track 4 on the CD while reading message silently or out loud. Play the music louder than usual to allow the vibrations of new creation to be in the foreground of your life.

There are many things I would like to accomplish, but to be honest, I would rather lie on the couch. I feel pulled toward avoiding the things that I would like to accomplish. While there have been many times in my life I have felt enthusiastic about getting things done, this is not one of those times. My energy is depleted, and I need a new birth and creation of the Energy of the Producer. I know that as I ask, I shall receive a new burst of vitality.

In this moment, I need the stimulation and the motivation of the Producer. The vibration of the Producer sets me into a rhythm where doing work and accomplishing my goals feels right in step with my everyday breathing and movement. When I am affected by the Producer Within, I do not have to push myself to work. In this state, working feels natural and is a lot of fun.

In this moment I listen to the music of the Producer and I can feel my body, mind, and spirit start to beat in rhythm with the rhythms of work and accomplishment.

I ask the Creator of All That Is to send me a new creation of this vibrant energy. While I have worked and accomplished my goals many times before, I need to begin again.

I allow my feet to tap and my body to move as I listen to the music of the Producer.

Message 12

The Producer-Still in the Essence Of

Listen to track 4 on the CD while reading message silently or out loud. Play the music at a normal volume.

Up and at 'em. The alarm goes off, and I am on my way. Quick coffee, shower, dress, and out the door. On my way: Get to work and work, work. "Hello, how are ya? Don't work too hard today Sally." I always like seeing Sally in the morning. She has a smile on her face. God bless her. For all I know she fought with her kids last night and her old man never came home, but bless her, she has a smile on her face every day when I arrive at work. Sally's smile lifts my spirit. That smile, that lovely smile is like a rose in a snowstorm.

You know, if I didn't go to work, I would miss things like Sally's smile. In this moment I am appreciating that part of me that is the Producer. I give thanks that I have the ability to be productive. Sometimes I think about people who can't get out of bed, or can't walk out of their homes. I am grateful to be able to go to work.

I love my paycheck. I like what I can buy and I don't even mind paying my bills. I am glad that I have bills to pay. I guess that means I have a life.

And when I "work at home" I am grateful to be serving my family and myself.

I am grateful that I am energetic. I am grateful that I have a life. I am also grateful that I relax at the end of the day. I think they call that a "balanced life."

As I listen to the music of the Producer, I bask in the productive energy that the music exudes. I take the time to immerse myself in the Energy of the Producer so that I may appreciate its special place within me.

Message 13

The Voter-Moving Toward

Listen to track 5 on the CD while reading message silently or out loud. Play the music at normal volume.

In this moment I need to move toward making a decision. Sitting on the fence will not do at this time. While I know that there will be those in my life who will not approve of my decision, I cannot let my fear of disapproval keep me from making a decision and placing "my vote" on the table.

The Voter Within calls out to be heard. The Voter knows that ultimately I will feel better about myself and find true inner satisfaction if I stop trying to please everyone and take a stand. How will I feel if I avoid expressing my opinion and let others make all the decisions? I cannot allow myself to avoid making decisions.

Yes, there will be those who may be upset with me, but there will also be those who will applaud my point of view. But even if I have to stand alone in this situation, I must not avoid the responsibility of making a choice.

As I listen to the music of the Voter, I feel encouraged to be brave and cast my lot for good or for worse. I am moving forward and into the Energy of the Voter.

Message 14

The Voter-Retreating From

Listen to track 5 on the CD while reading message silently or out loud. Play at a soft volume, as this is an energy you are retreating from and want to be background music in your life at this time.

At this time I need to step back and avoid making a decision. While there are many times in life that making a decision and casting my vote is the right thing to do, this is not one of those times.

So many decisions have been made and so much has happened. My body needs a rest. My mind needs a rest. My soul needs a rest. The Voter Within has been very active and too busy. Now it is time to rest and let my mind become at peace once again.

As I listen to the music of the Voter, I am pleased that I have been able to make so many decisions. I give grateful thanks to the Voter for the vibrations and energies of decision making that have been so important. With great thanks I say a temporary good-bye to the Voter and ask that the Creator of All That Is help me take the mental break that is needed so much at this time.

As I listen to the music and sit in contemplation, thoughts of relaxing activities come to mind. The music of the Voter fades into the background of my life.

Message 15

The Voter-Birth and Creation

*Listen to track 5 on the CD while reading message silently
or out loud. Play the music louder than usual to allow the
vibrations of new creation to be in the foreground of your life.*

I have taken stands on many issues in my life. I have also been willing to express my opinions on issues within my community. I have exercised the part of me that is the Voter. Now there is a feeling of exhaustion within my heart and soul that lets me know that if I am to continue to make decisions in my life I need a rebirth of that part of me that is the Voter.

I ask the Creator of All That Is to give me new energy at this time. As I listen to the music of the Voter, I can feel the exhaustion beginning to lift. A new vibration is stirring as I allow a new creation of the Voter to flow through my being. I feel exhilarated. I believe in being a participant in my life and in the lives of those around me. My personal world and the greater world around me need decisive people, and I want to be a full participant.

As I contemplate the vibrations of the Voter, I know that soon I will be able to participate in important decisions and I will be rested and ready to do so. I give grateful thanks for this new creation of the Voter Within.

Message 16

The Voter-Still in the Essence Of

Listen to track 5 on the CD while reading message silently or out loud. Play the music at normal volume.

I am the Voter. I am able to make a decision and then stand up and be counted. There are many issues in the world and in my own life where decisions are called for. The part of me that is the Voter will not stand for a wishy-washy approach to life. The Voter insists that I take a stand and stick by my decision with fierce loyalty.

In this moment, I am appreciating that part of myself that is the Voter. In this moment I do not need to make any decisions. I am free to contemplate that part of me that is the Voter.

Making choices is not always easy in our complex world, as there are such good arguments on each side of an issue. But if I want to make a difference in this world, I have to be involved in the choices of my own life, of the local community, my country, and my world. As the Voter, I listen to all sides of an issue, weigh the pros and cons, and then make a choice.

As I listen to the music of the Voter, I bask in the vibrations of this Energy. I feel like a member of a marching band of musicians. The music carries me along and lets me know that I am a participant. I am involved instead of shirking my responsibilities off to everyone else. I give grateful thanks to the Creator of All That Is for my ability to participate and be involved in life.

Message 17

The Warrior-Moving Toward

Listen to track 6 on the CD while reading message silently or out loud. Play the music at a normal volume.

Frustration has been my middle name lately. It seems that everything I plan falls apart and ends up going in the opposite direction. I am afraid to have any expectations about what will happen next. In this moment I need to call the Energy Within that is the Warrior.

The Warrior Within knows that having expectations is futile, as life does not happen the way we expect it to happen. The Warrior knows that I must Let Go and Let God. In this sense, letting God is letting that aspect of me that is the Warrior arise and cope with any situation that occurs. The Warrior is one of the many gifts I have received from the Creator of All That Is.

In this moment, I am not in touch with the aspect of me that is capable of surviving anything that happens. In this moment I could let my feelings of disappointment and frustration run my life. Or I have the free will to learn from this moment.

Let me take this moment as an opportunity. I call to the Warrior Within and ask that I move toward that energetic vibration that is capable of coping with all situations.

As I listen to the music of the Warrior, I choose to learn instead of giving into feeling sorry for myself. I choose to accept life as the rich tapestry of experiences that it is. And as I accept the tapestry of life with its many colors and situations, I am free.

As I listen to the music of the Warrior I contemplate faith and hope, strength and courage, knowing that the Creator is with me and part of me. I hear that the music plays on, the voice of life pauses now and again, taking a deep breath and continuing on.

Message 18

The Warrior-Retreating From

Listen to track 6 on the CD while reading message silently or out loud. Play at a soft volume, as this is an energy you are retreating from and want to be background music in your life at this time.

I need to retreat from the role of the Warrior. I have been fighting too many battles lately, and I need a rest. I need to retreat from the Energy of the Warrior, knowing very well that whatever issues and problems exist can be coped with at another time.

There is great exhaustion within my being because I have been wasting most of my energy trying to control life. And so in this time of exhaustion, I retreat from all thoughts of fighting. I must pay attention to this exhaustion and receive its warnings with gratitude.

When I am rested I will be ready once again to call on the Warrior and to face and survive whatever issues need attention in my life.

Everyone needs a time out once in awhile, and unless I am in a situation where to wait would bring disastrous results, I will step back now and rest. Movement is not my friend in this moment. Stillness is. As I am able to let go of control and call acceptance to my side, I notice that I am relaxing.

As I listen to the music of the Warrior, I let go of all thoughts of movement. I rest and I rest and I rest.

Message 19

The Warrior-Birth and Creation

Listen to track 6 on the CD while reading message silently or out loud. Play the music louder than usual to allow the vibrations of new creation to be in the foreground of your life.

My ability to cope with what life brings me is not great at this time. I find myself in need of a new burst of energy. While I am normally able to cope with most of life's situations, in this moment I feel that I cannot withstand one more complication in my life. This has been a time when I have had to cope with too much in a short period of time, and yet I must keep coping. My physical, emotional, and spiritual resources are at an all-time low. Life and its problems will not stop just because I am feeling depleted. I ask the Creator of All That Is to bring a new creation of the survival Energy to me. I ask for a new creation of the Warrior so that I will be ready to cope with whatever challenges life brings my way.

As I open my heart and soul, I realize that life has many beginnings and many endings. In this moment, I am experiencing a new beginning, and I feel the role of the Warrior penetrating my consciousness. A new and vibrant energy is flowing through me and around me. As I listen to the music of the Warrior I can feel the exhaustion lifting with every beat of the music. As I listen to the music of the Warrior, I feel the thrill of new creation and birth.

I give grateful thanks for every day that I live on this Earth. I am humble as I take each breath of life, knowing that life is a treasure. As I listen to the music, I contemplate and meditate on the new survival energy that I am receiving.

Message 20

The Warrior-Still in the Essence Of
Listen to track 6 on the CD while reading message silently or out loud. Play the music at normal volume.

When I am able to take life as it comes, and accept that I cannot control everything that happens, I am able to live a life both rich and spiritual. Even though there is much in my life that I can control, there are many circumstances that are unexpected. If I try to control every minute of my life, it is not possible and a waste of my precious energy.

I am the Warrior, as I am able to take life as it comes and do the best I can with whatever life brings my way. I turn to the Warrior to cope with anything that happens. In this moment I am basking in the vibrations of the Warrior Energy and appreciate that part of myself. In this moment when there is no battle to fight, it is nice to have a moment to sit and contemplate the wonder of the Energy of the Warrior.

The Warrior is able to survive all circumstances and knows which action to take depending on the moment. Sometimes surviving means that I give into resting when I am not feeling well. Sometimes surviving means fighting for an ideal that must be fought for. Surviving can mean many actions, depending on the particular circumstances life brings.

As I listen to the music of the Warrior, I am grateful to be alive and to have the opportunity to take on the challenges that living brings. I focus on the flexibility of the Warrior to react to each circumstance in a different manner, depending on what is needed in the moment.

I do not live in fear, as I am the Warrior.

Message 21

The Nurturer-Moving Toward

Listen to track 7 on the CD while reading message silently or out loud. Play the music at a normal volume.

I have not been taking care of myself in the ways I know are for my highest good. There are things that I have been doing that I know are not the best for my body, mind, and spirit. In this moment, I ask the Creator of All That Is to move me toward taking greater care of myself. I call to that aspect of my being that is the Nurturer.

Knowing what to do to nurture myself is sometimes confusing. Each day I learn more and more about things that I can do to take better care of myself. Knowing that no one soul has all the time, money, and know-how to do everything the experts suggest, I now ask for the vibrations of reason and logic to guide me in the choices I need to make about how to best take care of myself. I also ask my heart and soul to take part in decisions of nurturing myself.

As I listen to the music of the Nurturer, the natural sway of the music and the easy flow of the melody bring relaxation and comfort. In this moment, I realize that taking care of myself *is* natural and *can* be easygoing if I will only bring an attitude of relaxation to my everyday life. The music helps to guide me toward this relaxed attitude. I am moving forward and into the Energy of the Nurturer.

As I listen to the music, I meditate and contemplate and accept that taking care of myself as well as others is a natural part of living. I also know that taking care of the planet Earth is part of the job of the Nurturer. I am grateful for the Nurturer Within, one of the many gifts of the Creator.

Message 22

The Nurturer-Retreating From

Listen to track 7 on the CD while reading silently or out loud.
Play at a soft volume, as this is an energy you are retreating
from and want to be background music in your life at this time.

I have been overly involved with the part of myself that is the Nurturer, and I need to step back. Too many of my thoughts are concerned with my problems, the problems of others, or the problems of the world.

Where have the carefree times gone? Where are those moments of total relaxation where I do not feel a care or worry? Where are the laughter, the song, and the dance of my life?

Am I so busy taking care of everything that comes into my path that I am losing the joy of living? Am I so obsessed with taking care of myself that I am not allowing myself to have any fun?

As I listen to the music of the Nurturer, I am reminded that nurturing myself, others, and my world should be a natural part of my life and not a part of life that becomes obsessive and anxiety producing. In this moment I realize that it is not good for me to spend so much time investigating every possible way to nurture myself. Right now I need to clear my mind of all thoughts and just relax.

In this moment I meditate on restoring balance to my life.

Message 23

The Nurturer-Birth and Creation

Listen to track 7 on the CD while reading message silently or out loud. Play the music louder than usual to allow the vibrations of new creation to be in the foreground of your life.

I am tired of nurturing myself. I am tired of taking care of myself and the others in my life. While I have done a pretty good job, and I give grateful thanks to the Nurturer Within, the truth is, in this moment I need a new creation of the vibration I know as the Nurturer. There is part of me that would like to abandon all the good ways I take care of myself and the others in my life. But I know that taking care of myself is something I must do for a lifetime. In this moment, I ask for a new birth and creation of the vibration of the Nurturer. I need new energy at this time.

I know the Creator is providing me with what I need in this moment. I need the fire of motivation to be rekindled. As I open my heart and soul, I receive. As I listen to the music of the Nurturer, I can feel the vibrations of new vital energy pouring into my being. This is a gift of the Creator.

As I listen to the music, I am allowing my breathing to slow and deepen. It feels good to be in touch with my inner soul once again and to know that I can get what I need. I can take care of myself. I can help others.

Message 24

The Nurturer-Still in the Essence Of

Listen to track 7 on the CD while reading message silently or out loud. Play the music at a normal volume.

I know that taking care of myself is *the* most important thing in my life. As a spiritual being, I realize that my soul lives in a vehicle called "the physical body," which has within it, among others parts, a brain and a heart. It is the Nurturer Within that takes care of all of me.

In this moment I take the time to appreciate the part of me that is the Nurturer. I immerse myself in this vibration and give thanks.

I not only have a body, but I have a soul. But can these elements really be separate from each other? I think not. In this moment, I experience that every part of my being, every aspect of who I am, is part of the Creator of All That Is. While I am an individual, I am part of the Divine Whole of Creation. The Nurturer Within is a gift of the Creator. This aspect of my being takes care of me.

The Nurturer aspect of my individuality is also able to take care of others in my family, my community, and my world. This is as it should be, as I am part of all that exists. I am also able to do my part in taking care of the land, the sky, and the sea.

"What a huge job," my mind cries. "I cannot take care of so much!" But my soul knows that each soul is part of the Creator of All Existence. When any one of us allows the Nurturer Within to do its work, the Nurturer within the individual soul joins with the Energy of the Nurturer that is part of the Creator. No one does the job alone.

Message 25

The Seeker-Moving Toward

Listen to track 8 on the CD while reading message silently or out loud. Play at a normal volume.

The voices of all time have been calling to me. The eyes of my soul are seeing, the ears of my soul are hearing, and the essence of my soul is sensing all that has ever been. The mystical journey is deep and multidimensional. There is a knowing that in this moment the Seeker is going to move forward on the mystical journey.

I am pulled forward in my journey, and I move deeper and deeper at a slow and steady pace, needing time to absorb each new vibration that I encounter on the path. There is no need to hurry, for to hurry would create a frantic path where I would surely fall and stumble, missing all the knowledge on the path and of the path. The Seeker Within knows how to move forward on a smooth and gentle vibration.

As I move deeper, it sometimes seems hard to return to the normal state of consciousness within which I lead my everyday life. I want to remain in the mystical forces that bring such light to me. I want to receive more and more from the Seeker.

But in my knowing, I understand that part of moving forward within the mystical is the bringing back of the knowledge to make daily life meaningful. As I move forward in the mystical journey, I know that coming back to a normal state of consciousness is part of the mystical journey, because it is in my everyday life that I share the love the soul has to offer.

As I listen to the music of the Seeker, I meditate on moving forward and deeper into the mystical journey. I contemplate finding balance in my life within the mystical.

Message 26

The Seeker-Retreating From

Listen to track 8 on the CD while reading message silently or out loud. Play at a soft volume, as this is an energy you are retreating from and want to be background music in your life at this time.

My head is swimming, and dizziness takes over the essence of all that I am. The voices of my soul are calling to me and telling me it is time to withdraw from the mystical state of consciousness and return to the ordinary tasks that daily life presents. The mystical journey must fade into the background of my life for a while. It is time to sweep the floor, take out the garbage, wash the car, do errands, and talk to the people of my everyday life. The balance in my life has been lost. I am out of balance and need to once again find the status quo of my everyday existence.

In this moment I ask that aspect of me that is the Seeker to retreat for a while so that I can take care of practical responsibilities.

Let me in this moment give in to the need to let go of all mystical pursuits and thoughts of my spiritual progress. Let me focus on what to cook for dinner, the need to do the laundry, and the exercise I need. I learn that it is in balance that I find true spirituality. And so I am grateful that the mystical path is giving me the message that I need to retreat and withdraw for the moment.

As I listen to the music of the Seeker, I let this music flow into the background of my life. Saying good-bye to the Seeker is not for long, and once rested I will be ready again to continue the mystical journey.

Message 27

The Seeker-Birth and Creation

Listen to track 8 on the CD while reading message silently or out loud. Play the music louder than usual to allow the vibrations of new creation to be in the foreground of your life.

In this moment I feel a new energy building within the part of me that is the Seeker. My inner spirit yearns to explore a new mystical path, and so I pay attention to the callings of my soul and allow the new path to begin in this moment. Vibrations of excitement begin to penetrate my body, mind, and spirit. I allow myself to experience the feelings of creation and movement.

In this moment I do not need to understand on an intellectual level all that is happening as I begin on this new mystical path. There have been times that my intellect has stamped out and destroyed the mystical paths that have been open to me. In this moment I am asking my intellectual side to remain quiet so that the voices of my soul may be heard clearly. I am asking the new vibration of the Seeker to guide me. This moment belongs to the purely mystical creation of the new path, which is unveiled before me at this time.

As I listen to the music of the Seeker, I am in wonderment as I feel the creativity that is taking place. I give thanks to the Creator of All That Is for this opportunity to explore the Divine.

Message 28

The Seeker-Still in the Essence Of

Listen to track 8 on the CD while reading message silently or out loud. Play the music at a normal volume.

The voices from the deep places of the Earth call to me. The voices from the universe lure me into the mystical journey of my soul. I am the Seeker who thirsts for knowledge of the mysteries of the universe.

As I am quiet and listen to the messages that come to me from near and far, the intrigue pulls me. I instinctively open my soul to the mystical path before me.

In this moment I am pausing to appreciate the part of me that is the Seeker and to give grateful thanks for this vibration. I am still in the essence of the mystical vibrations. As I listen to the music of the Seeker, I contemplate my mystical journey, and listen for the voices that speak to me. I listen to the voices of my soul.

How dull life is when there is no mystical journey. How boring it becomes for life to be three-dimensional when there are so many dimensions curving and evolving within each other. There is a whole matrix of planes and levels available to the Seeker who is willing to take the journey.

In this moment, my soul can hear the strains of music that come from the cosmos, intriguing and appealing in the veils of meaning that come sometimes slowly and pierce my heart with meaning. I give grateful thanks to the Creator of All That Is for the aspect of my being that is the Seeker.

Message 29

The Communicator-Moving Toward

Listen to track 9 on the CD while reading message silently or out loud. Play the music at a normal volume.

I feel all cooped up: tied up with thoughts and feelings that I can share with no one. Alone on an island with my thoughts, I feel a stranger to all I meet. It is not that I always feel this way. There are times when I am able to share my thoughts with someone who truly hears me, and it is beautiful music that plays through me as I express myself. But in this moment, the part of me that is the Communicator is struggling. I need to move forward and into the Energy of the Communicator.

In this moment I call to the Communicator Within to gently help me be more expressive. As I feel the vibration of the Communicator, my breathing becomes steady and deep. I can feel my throat relaxing. I am grateful for the gentle vibration of this aspect of my being.

As I listen to the Communicator Within, I hear, "Risk to the rescue! I must learn to take more risks and allow myself greater expression."

There are many ways I can express myself. I can talk to people, write letters, and attend support groups. I can write music, write poetry, paint, and make sculpture. Communication is a many-faceted friend. Self-expression can free me and release me.

As I listen to the music of the Communicator, I know that I am steadily moving toward greater self-expression.

Message 30

The Communicator-Retreating From

Listen to track 9 on the CD while reading message silently or out loud. Play the music softly, as this is an energy you are retreating from and want to be background music in your life right now.

Have I been talking too much? Yes, I have. Not only are the people in my life tired of hearing me, but also I am tired of hearing my own voice. While I know that expressing my thoughts and feelings is important, right now my life is out of balance. It's funny how all great things live on a fine line. There is a fine line between not expressing myself enough and expressing myself too much. It is often hard for me to find that fine line. When I find it, my relationships are very comfortable and enjoyable. When I express myself too little, I feel all cooped up inside and separated from those I love. And then when I express myself too much, as I have lately, I feel exhausted, as do my loved ones who have been listening to me.

In this moment I call to that aspect of my being that is the Communicator and respectfully request that we take a much-needed break! Knowing that there is a time and a place for everything, I know in this moment that this is the proper time to retreat from self-expression. This is a time to quiet my thoughts and to subdue my feelings and rest.

As I listen to the music of the Communicator, I say a temporary farewell and prepare myself to rest in silence. In this moment, it is in silence that I will find peace.

Message 31

The Communicator-Birth and Creation

Listen to track 9 on the CD while reading message silently or out loud. Play the music louder than usual to allow the vibrations of new creation to be in the foreground of your life.

I am changing as the winds change their direction, as the seeds of flowers mutate over the ages and produce new kinds of flowers. I am unfolding, and the vibrations within me are changing their pace and changing their rhythm. The colors of my soul are not the same as they used to be. All is new and different and I am born anew to this world.

I receive. The Creator of All That Is brings a new creation of the Communicator Within. I am on a new journey, and I receive new and vital vibrations.

The way I express myself no longer suits me. While the very heart and soul of what I call "myself" has transformed, I am still expressing myself in terms of the old me. I still talk the same way, walk the same way, and gesture the same way. My physical and mental bodies have not yet caught up with the changes of my inner spirit, my soul.

I am asking the Creator of All That Is to create within me new forms of expression, and I am receiving. I ask that I may integrate within my being all that is part of my being.

As I listen to the music of the Communicator, I can feel the vibrations of new expression flowing through my being. I allow this transformation to take place in this moment.

I meditate and contemplate the changes that have taken place within, and as I sit with myself, I feel the integration of the physical, mental, and spiritual bodies taking place.

Message 32

The Communicator-Still in the Essence Of

Listen to track 9 on the CD while reading message silently or out loud. Play the music at normal volume.

Expression, communication: the serious and the trivial images within. All the many images that play through my mind are there to be communicated. The images that dwell deep within my subconscious mind are there to be retrieved and expressed. And the sweetness of the soul that existed long before this body was born is calling to my soul.

In this moment, I am aware of that aspect of my being that is the Communicator. I am immersed in the essence of the Communicator. I take time now to appreciate this energy that lives within me.

Expression is a choice I make every day: my thoughts are to be or not to be expressed. Oh, there are so many opinions about expression. "Let all your feelings out!" "Don't be a complainer." "Always tell the truth." "Don't wear your heart on your sleeve." Many of the arguments between people are about what someone did or did not express. Most of the misunderstandings revolve around the way someone said something.

Communication: the world of the bitter and the sweet. And yet when expression works well, it is the mighty river that flows majestically through the valley; it is the sunset with glorious colors; it is the smell of the grass and flowers after the rain.

In this moment I am aware that the Communicator Within makes wise decisions about the way I express myself to others each day. The Communicator helps me find balance in the expression of my thoughts and feelings.

As I listen to the music of the Communicator, I contemplate self-expression, knowing that I am growing in my ability to express myself.

Message 33

The Lover-Moving Toward

Listen to track 10 on the CD while reading message silently or out loud. Play the music at a normal volume.

I ask the Creator of All That Is to bring me to a place where I can feel the beauty of existence. At this time, my life is consumed with "I have to" and "I should." Once again I wish to experience those moments when time stops and I feel the beauty of life all around me. In my present state of mind, I am not allowing the beauty of life to be the prominent force in my life. In this moment, I call to that aspect of my being that is the Lover.

A sadness flows through my heart and soul as I think of the beauty I am missing at this time. Although I know that life is eternal and when I give up my earthly body, I will continue on in the world of spirit, I also know that life in this body, on this Earth is wondrous. I want to experience its beauty *now.*

As I listen to the music of the Lover, I can feel the walls of practicality that I have built around myself crumbling. As these energies of "Do this and do that" fall away, the sweet sounds of beauty enter my soul. I begin to feel playful and adventurous.

In my mind's eye I see myself flying across the sky over mountaintops and valleys, touching the clouds as I fly. Oh, great freedom, you are entering my soul once again.

As I listen to the music, I contemplate and meditate on the freeing of my soul once again. I am becoming again, the Lover of Life.

Message 34

The Lover-Retreating From

Listen to track 10 on the CD while reading message silently or out loud. Play the music softly, as this is an energy you are retreating from and want to be background music in your life right now.

I am the Lover, the Lover of Life. I am having a wonderful time, finding beauty in all that comes my way. In this moment, I love the people I see around me, and I am having more fun than I have ever had. The problem is, I am so involved with this aspect of my being that is the Lover that I can't seem to find the time to come back to Earth and do things like clean my house and pay my bills. Why would anyone want to do the mundane things in life, when one is having so much fun?

Fortunately, the vibration within that often calls itself "common sense" is calling to me at this moment. I am hearing loud and clear that I need to pull back momentarily from the beauty of life in order to take care of the practical, material challenges in my life. Going to the dentist and such are important! In this moment I call to that aspect of my being that is the Lover and ask that this part of myself retreat for a short while.

As I listen to the music of the Lover, I commit myself to taking care of some practical tasks that the Lover Within does not necessarily enjoy doing.

In this moment, I am grateful that I have the ability to be the Lover, and I know that while I may need to retreat to more mundane tasks for the moment, I will return soon to that part of me that can fly and play and spin.

Message 35

The Lover-Birth and Creation

Listen to track 10 on the CD while reading message silently or out loud. Play the music louder than usual to allow the vibrations of new creation to be in the foreground of your life.

In this moment I begin again. I am expanding and feeling the intense beauty of existence.

There have been many times in my life when I have been happy and open to the joy of life. There have been other times when I have been weighted down by all the challenges daily life brings.

I am exhausted from taking care of my life. I need a new creation of the Energy of the Lover. I do not wish to allow my exhaustion to lead me into negative thinking or depression. I will rise above exhaustion as I ask the Creator for new birth and creation of the Energy of the Lover.

The Creator of All That Exists brings me in this moment to a place where I am being born again into the joy of life. I can feel the exhaustion lifting. I am experiencing a new creation of that aspect of my being that is the Lover.

As I listen to the music of the Lover, I can sway to the music and begin to feel the vibrations of excitement flow through my being. There is an energy expanding within me that I have never experienced before. As I listen to the music, my heart and soul are open to joy.

Message 36

The Lover-Still in the Essence Of

Listen to track 10 on the CD while reading message silently or out loud. Play the music at a normal volume.

I am the Lover. I am the Lover of Life. I allow my romantic nature to surface, and I experience the wonderment of life. I am the Lover in everything I do. I love the land, the trees on the land, the sea, and the fish in the sea, the sky and the birds that fly the sky. I love all of humanity and the animal kingdom. In a romantic relationship, I am able to give myself fully to the Lover Within. When I am the friend, my friendships are joyful and compassionate.

In this moment, I am the Lover, the Lover of Life, and I allow myself to find the beauty in all that exists. I take the time now to appreciate and experience the essence of the Energy of the Lover.

Pools of beauty flood my eyes as I clearly allow my soul to see with the spiritual eyes of the Lover. Colors change and expand and swirl before me. As I allow the colors of life to swirl, my very being expands and that which was before changes into a glow of golden light.

As I listen to the music of the Lover, I feel the playful rhythms. I become the voice of the Lover of Life, flowing and changing, finding my way into all the nooks and crannies of existence. My essence flows through matter into the spheres of the subtleties of beauty. I immerse myself in and contemplate the nature of the Lover.

As I listen to the music, the consciousness that I call "mine" becomes linked with the greater cosmic consciousness of All That Is.

Message 37

The Peacemaker-Moving Toward

Listen to track 11 on the CD while reading message silently or out loud. Play the music at a normal volume.

Making peace is not easy for me in this moment. I resist making peace with those in my life who have caused me trouble. But is it really trouble that has been brought into my life, or learning? Have I not learned from these difficult experiences that we are all different souls with different viewpoints? Why do I assume that those who do not follow my view of life are wrong?

I am moving forward and toward the Energy of the Peacemaker. Today, I am not ready to make peace with those I have been in conflict with. I call to the Peacemaker Within to bring the vibrations of peacemaking to my heart and soul so that I may move toward resolving and dissipating the conflicts within.

I am moving toward real peace—not the superficial peace that speaks the words of peace without there being any true resolution on the soul level.

I understand fully that to make peace with those I disagree with is not to condone their ideas or behaviors if they are opposed to my values. I ask only to make peace within my own heart and soul, so that I am not weighted with the heaviness of anger. I wish to let my grudges go and feel light again.

As I listen to the music of the Peacemaker, I allow myself to let the feelings of peace flow within my being.

Message 38

The Peacemaker-Retreating From

Listen to track 11 on the CD while reading message silently or out loud. Play the music softly, as this is an energy you are retreating from and want to be background music in your life right now.

I have been the "peacemaker" in my circle of family and friends. But as I am taking an honest look at my behavior, I realize I am creating an atmosphere where no real peace can take place. I am smoothing over situations where people should have open discussions in order to bring their feelings out into the open. Even though open discussions may bring uncomfortable conflict, these discussions need to take place.

I have been trying to act as a peacemaker and actually creating a war zone of superficial compliance. People are acting as if they are at peace while real feelings of anger exist below the surface of the apparently calm waters. Eventually the calm surface will show the disruptive feelings from within. I will not try to make peace in a superficial manner any longer.

I am tired of trying to make peace between people. As I listen to the music of the Peacemaker, I am realizing that there are times I need to step back, mind my own business, and let others make their own peace with each other.

As I listen to the music of the Peacemaker, I step back from the Energy I know as the Peacemaker.

Message 39

The Peacemaker-Birth and Creation

Listen to track 11 on the CD while reading message silently or out loud. Play the music louder than usual to allow the vibrations of new creation to be in the foreground of your life.

Life unfolds in stages. I am able to attain a certain level of expertise with every aspect of my being. In this moment I realize I am ready to expand in the aspect of my being that I know as the Peacemaker.

As I contemplate my portfolio of emotional, physical, and spiritual vibrations, I ask the Creator of All That Is to create new vibrations of peace within my heart and soul. I ask for a new beginning on the pathway of peace. I ask for a new creation of the Peacemaker.

While I have been able to make peace with many people in my life, there is a desire to experience the vibrations of peacemaking in a new and more meaningful manner. I wish to have more wisdom and better judgment as I endeavor to make peace within myself, peace with others, and peace between others. In the past I have acted as a peacemaker when I should have stepped back and let others work out their own difficulties. I have robbed others of their own responsibilities. I ask the Creator for a new birth and creation of that Energy which I know as the Peacemaker. I ask that I become more successful in my abilities to know when to act as a Peacemaker and when to step back.

In this moment, I allow myself to experience the new birth of the Peacemaker. As I listen to the music of the Peacemaker, I feel new energy of peace flowing into my being. I am grateful and I give thanks.

Message 40

The Peacemaker-Still in the Essence Of

Listen to track 11 on the CD while reading message silently or out loud. Play the music at a normal volume.

I am the Peacemaker. This aspect of my being wants to make peace in life where there have been difficulties. The Peacemaker Within wants to move toward a solution and create peace where there are disagreements. I am grateful for the Energy of the Peacemaker, and I allow the vibrations of this Energy to penetrate my being.

In this moment I immerse myself in the Energy of the Peacemaker and appreciate this part of myself.

The Peacemaker Within encourages me to let go of anger and send grudges off into the ethers. The Peacemaker knows that no one is perfect and encourages me to accept imperfection in myself and in others. The Peacemaker merges with the vibration of forgiveness. This aspect of my being lets me see that as I hold onto anger toward another, it is really anger toward myself that I am carrying around. The anger I hold toward another human being is reflected in the mirror of my own being. As I judge another, so I judge myself. As I allow myself to let go and forgive, my whole being feels light again.

As I listen to the music, I allow myself to be drawn into the vibrations of the Eternal Peacemaker, knowing that I am in the process of making peace with all of existence. I contemplate the nature of the Peacemaker and give thanks.

Message 41

The Devotee-Moving Toward

Listen to track 12 on the CD while reading message silently or out loud. Play the music at a normal volume.

In this moment, I move toward the essence of devotion. I feel scattered, and my direction does not seem clear.

There are times when I find the concept of being devoted to anything unappealing. Sometimes I have an image of those who are devoted as uneducated followers who cannot make any decisions for themselves. This is not the kind of devotion I wish to practice.

On the other hand, there are also the devoted beings who make a soulful search into spirituality and have chosen a spiritual path after much contemplation. Once they make a choice they have the spiritual strength to be consistently devoted. This is the kind of devotion I am moving toward.

In this moment, I call to that aspect of my being that is the Devotee. I am moving toward a greater acceptance of that part of my being that needs the life of spiritual devotion.

I realize that devotion has many forms. One may be devoted to a spiritual master, a way of living, or a set of ideas. Devotion is not always practiced by attending a house of worship or meditating. Some people receive the gifts of devotion as they write, paint, or compose music. Some find the path of devotion within scientific discovery. There are many paths of devotion.

As I listen to the music of the Devotee, I am moving forward and into the vibrations of the Devotee. I move toward allowing myself to make a choice in my spiritual path of devotion.

In this moment, as I move toward the Devotee, I do so with the understanding that there are many ways for me to experience this vibration.

Message 42

The Devotee-Retreating From

Listen to track 12 on the CD while reading message silently or out loud. Play the music softly, as this is an energy you are retreating from and want to be background music in your life right now.

In this moment I need to step back from the Devotee Within. I have been involved in the aspects of devotion in my life to the point where other aspects of my being are ignored. While so absorbed in that part of me that is the Devotee I have not been paying enough attention to the Producer, the Nurturer, and the Voter. I need to work and take care of business. I need to take care of my physical being, and I need to be available to make the decisions each day that my life requires.

Sometimes I can get lost in the ecstasy of devotional practices and I do not want to allow any other aspects of my being into my consciousness. This creates a lack of balance.

As I listen to the music of the Devotee I begin to retreat from the mystical, magical, and ecstatic feelings that my devotion sometimes brings. I do this with the understanding that to become totally absorbed in devotional practices and to let one's everyday life go uncared for is a misuse of devotion.

In this moment, I am retreating from the Devotee; I do so knowing that I am not giving up the Devotee Within. I am only pulling back in this moment in order to make room for other important aspects of my being. The Devotee will still be an important part of my life but will not consume all of my life energy.

Message 43

The Devotee-Birth and Creation

Listen to track 12 on the CD while reading message silently or out loud. Play the music louder than usual to allow the vibrations of new creation to be in the foreground of your life.

I pray to the Creator of All That Is to hear me in this moment. This is a special moment in my life in which I am asking for a rebirth of the Devotee Within. I long for and know that I am ready to receive a new Energy that will allow me to be involved in devotional practices on a deeper level than I have ever experienced.

I know that the Devotee Within is connected to the Supreme Being, and I yearn to have a deeper connection to the Divine. I ask for the vibrations of new and deeper spiritual growth. The mystery of the soul opens to me as I ask for the birth of new energy.

As I listen to the music of the Devotee, I receive the gifts of the spiritual world. In this moment I am receiving the new creation of the Devotee. Thoughts leave my mind and I experience sensations within my being that are vital and intense. As the Energy flows within me, it is also peaceful and serene. In this moment, I do not try to understand. I only absorb.

I listen to the music and allow myself to be enveloped within this beautiful Energy. A warm glow fills my being.

Message 44

The Devotee-Still in the Essence Of

Listen to track 12 on the CD while reading message silently or out loud. Play the music at a normal volume.

I feel the Energy and vibrations of the Devotee. The sweet strains of these influences flow through my being like the gently falling rain. The strong influences of these vibrations flow as the waters of the great oceans and rivers. The powers of my devotion rise in the sky as great mountain ranges. I am in touch with that aspect of myself that is the Devotee.

The golden glow of devotion finds its rightful place in my heart. As I center my conscious thoughts on my heart, I can feel the glow of my devotion carrying me into realms of consciousness that distract me from my daily life and conscious thoughts.

I am taking the time to appreciate and be still in the essence of the Energy of the Devotee.

As I listen to the music of the Devotee, I allow the peaceful cadence of the music to carry me into the realms of the inner soul, the seat of my devotion. Music is vibration, and the music carries me into the mysteries of my devotional practice.

As I allow myself to flow into my devotion, there is a peace that goes beyond anything my conscious mind can understand. In this moment, I flow into the essence of my devotion and lose all sense of personal self. My being merges into the Great One.

In this moment the music washes over me and through me into stillness and peace.

Message 45

The Healer-Moving Toward

Listen to track 13 on the CD while reading message silently or out loud. Play the music at normal volume.

In the busyness of life, my energies have been separated from the healing available to me. I notice that there are pains in my body and disturbances in my mind. Right now, I am not able to help myself or others in my life as I would like. In this moment I call to that aspect of my being known as the Healer.

I ask the Creator of All Life to help me relax and once again allow the healing energies of the universe to penetrate my entire being. I am moving forward and into the Energy of the Healer.

Most of the crisis that develops in life is due to the rejection of the forces of healing. In this moment, I stop rejecting or closing out the healing energies. I open myself to healing. I move toward the Healer Within.

As I listen to the music of the Healer, I breathe deeply and can feel the chemistry of my body changing already. I feel my muscles relax and my mind clear. It is as if a healing breeze has just wrapped me in good feelings.

In this moment as I am moving toward healing, I am moving into that part of myself that allows me to open to the healing energies of the universe.

Message 46

The Healer-Retreating From

Listen to track 13 on the CD while reading message silently or out loud. Play the music softly, as this is an energy you are retreating from and want to be background music in your life right now.

While the true essence of healing can never be a problem or energy to withdraw from, I have been misusing the ideas and concepts of healing and therefore must withdraw from these false ideas. I have been trying to use my thoughts of healing as tools to control my own destiny or the destiny of another person. I have insisted that I heal immediately or that another person heal immediately, as if I had some kind of control.

The truth is, I am not in control of my destiny or the destiny or any other being.

When I pray for myself, I need to pray for whatever is for my highest good. When I pray for others, I need to pray for what is for the highest good of others.

I am not the judge of what is the highest good, and yet I have been setting myself up as that judge.

In this moment, I need to retreat from trying to heal myself. I have been overdoing it, and it is time to think of other things, and let the healing energy do its work. I need to get out of my own way. At this particular time when I have been so obsessive about healing, I may be preventing my own healing. I may heal faster if I am not thinking about it.

As I listen to the music of the Healer, I allow myself to feel the mystery of life and creation. I need to stop being insistent that I heal or that someone else heals. Life will take its course.

Message 47

The Healer-Birth and Creation

Listen to track 13 on the CD while reading message silently or out loud. Play the music louder than usual to allow the vibrations of new creation to be in the foreground of your life.

I ask in this moment for a new creation of the Healer. While my thoughts of healing and study of healing in the past has been beneficial, in this moment I am ready for the creation of a new level of ability that will allow healing to flow through my being more than ever before.

I am ready, like the student who has graduated one program, to begin a new program. This is a moment to begin anew as I become a clear channel for the healing of the universe. My excitement grows as I realize I am taking a step forward into the deeper mysteries of healing.

As I listen to the music of the Healer, my mind wanders to the great healers of ancient times, knowing that their energies still flow throughout the universe. These Spirits of Ancient Healing are able to send healing in waves throughout the universe to those who are in need.

In this moment, I am ready to accept on a higher level, the ability to channel healing for myself and others. With great reverence, I now open myself and allow myself to receive.

In this moment, I experience the birth of new healing energies within.

Message 48

The Healer-Still in the Essence Of

Listen to track 13 on the CD and read message silently or out loud. Play the music at a normal volume.

I am Spirit. We are all spirits living in physical bodies. The Spirit within each one of us is linked with all the dimensions of consciousness that are the essence of the universe. Our planet is a place for learning, where each one of us incarnates into a physical body, to live a life for a brief moment in time.

Timeless is the universe at large, and each soul finding a way into a physical body breathes and lives in the physical for a short moment.

I take the time to appreciate and immerse myself in the Energy of the Healer. I give grateful thanks.

Healing is the answer to the questions living brings. Healing is the absence of fear and the recognition of a power greater than each one of us. Healing is the essence of love, and love is the dynamic force upon which existence and the continuity of existence are founded.

The Healer is that aspect of my being that brings peace to my mind, body, and spirit. The Healer Within is that aspect of me that brings health when there is illness, happiness when there is sorrow.

In this moment I recognize and experience once again that the Healer Within is that aspect of my being that is connected directly to the Creator of All That Is. I do not heal myself or others, but the Healer Within is able to channel the healing energy from the Divine Spirit. I give grateful thanks for the Healer.

PART 3

Working in Depth with the Process

Chapter 9

STOP, LOOK, AND LISTEN

The Psychic Intuitive Guidance Process will be of absolutely no use to you if you do not *remember* to use it. How many times in life do we learn about some great new way of thinking or managing our lives, and once we have read about it, we forget to *use* it? It becomes like so many kitchen utensils that sit in the kitchen drawer and never get used, or like never-worn clothes in the closet that just hang there taking up space.

The Stop, Look, and Listen technique will ensure that you use the Psychic Intuitive Guidance Process. This technique is as important as the process itself.

Stop, Look, and Listen

I was born in 1940. As I was growing up, there was an expression that kids were taught to say to themselves before crossing the street: "Stop, Look, and Listen." You stopped and looked to see if any cars were coming and listened also for any approaching cars. Then once you knew the coast was clear, you crossed the street.

Obviously, if you crossed the street before you stopped, looked, and listened, you might, in a split second, get hit and injured by an approaching car.

The other day I was thinking about how life can change in a second, how things happen in a split second that can change our lives and our moods. These are not usually as serious as getting hit by a car, but these split-second changes can alter anyone's day and ultimately their whole life.

For instance, if someone says something rude to me, all of a sudden I feel the energy within me change. Or I get some news about something that does not please me, and I can be in a different mood for hours or even for the rest of the day. It occurred to me that the greatest gift I can give myself at that moment is to *Stop, Look, and Listen.* I believe that this is also the greatest gift that you can give yourself. When we feel some kind of shift of energy, mood, or physical sensations, we need to access what is happening *immediately!* Just like a child who is learning to be safe when crossing the street, we need to *stop* before doing anything else and access what is happening. If we neglect to stop and do a mental survey of what is going on, our mood can sometimes change for the rest of the day. These days add up to weeks, months, and years, and before we know it years of dissatisfaction have accumulated.

Stop

When you feel a shift, *stop* what you are doing and check in with yourself. What just happened to cause the shift? Did someone say something to upset you? Did you just trip and hurt your knee? Did something happen that triggered a painful memory? Stop and check in. (Obviously, if you are in a situation where stopping would put you in some kind of danger, then keep doing whatever you have to in order to get out of danger. But for the most part in everyday life, we do have time to stop and check in.)

Stop and find out what is happening *right now.* If you wait until it is convenient, it may be too late to receive this wisdom that the current moment offers.

Look

Create a mental picture of your body. Do you feel pain or tension anywhere within your physical body? Does your stomach hurt? Does your head hurt, or do you feel like you are just about to get a headache?

Create a mental picture of your emotions. If you like, imagine an empty circle and ask your intuitive wisdom if you are emotionally upset. As you look into that circle, see if any words begin to appear. You may find that your inner guidance will actually spell out for you what is bothering you on a deep level. You may see the word *angry, sad,* or *fearful* appear in the circle. Or you may see words such as *anxious* or *depressed.*

Once you have stopped and looked, you will have some idea of what has caused your change of mood. Now it is time to *listen* with your intuitive ear to hear the inner guidance that is always available to you.

Listen

Ask your inner guidance to tell you which of the Twelve Energies you need to call upon at this moment. Also ask yourself which of the Four States of Being you need to combine with the Energy you have chosen. For instance, if you feel drawn to the Energy of the Healer, do you need to move toward this Energy, retreat from this Energy, experience the true essence of this Energy, or ask for a new creation of this Energy?

If you have the time, sit and read the message that goes with the Energy and State of Being you have intuitively chosen. If you do not have the time, then reflect for a few moments on the Energy and State of Being. Once you are familiar with the Energies and the

Four States of Being, you can call on them anywhere, any time. You will not always have to work with the messages and the CD.

Change Your Mood in a Matter of Moments

Here is an example of how the Stop, Look, and Listen tool can work for you. Let's say that you have just had a conversation with a friend who has done nothing but complain for thirty minutes. You have tried to help your friend, but no matter what you suggest, she continues to feel that nothing will help her. You notice that you are feeling drained and exhausted as you get off the phone. You *stop* and acknowledge that you are feeling depleted. Next you *look*. You scan your body, and you notice that your back hurts and you are beginning to get a headache. You assess your emotions and notice that you are feeling frustrated and resentful. You are both frustrated with your friend for being so negative and frustrated with yourself for spending so much time on the phone call when you were not doing either one of you any good.

Next you *listen*. Ask your intuitive inner guidance which of the Twelve Energies you need. The Energy that comes to mind immediately is that of the Nurturer. Then you ask for the State of Being and immediately hear "Retreat From." You open the book and read the message for the Nurturer-Retreating From. You turn on the CD and play the music of the Nurturer softly, as this is an Energy you now want in the background of your life. As you focus on the message and the music, you realize that you are not going to give this negative friend so much attention anymore. Your body relaxes, and the headache never develops.

Next you feel drawn to reading the message of the Nurturer-Moving Toward, and you realize that in *this* moment it is yourself you need to nurture. You read the message and play the music at a higher volume, as you want this Energy in the forefront of your life.

You have not only changed your mood in a matter of minutes, but you have come to some important conclusions about your relationship with this friend, conclusions that will help you as the days go on.

Two weeks later you are in the grocery store and this same friend approaches you. Suddenly your mind flashes on the experience you had with the message of the Nurturer-Retreating From. The feelings that you experienced while reading the message and listening to the music are instantly retrieved. You realize you need to be careful with this friend right now. You are polite and friendly, but you do not get overly involved in the conversation. Three minutes later, the conversation is over. You feel rested and do not have any guilt.

Using the Stop, Look, and Listen technique will help you get the most out of the Psychic Intuitive Guidance Process, as it will help you to remember to use the process when you have a problem or a change of mood.

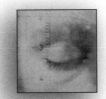

Chapter 10

TIPS ON WORKING
IN DEPTH WITH THE PROCESS

I suggest that you use the Psychic Intuitive Guidance Process several times as you have been instructed to do in previous chapters. Then, when you've had some experience with the process, read this chapter to learn how to get the most out of your experiences with the Psychic Intuitive Guidance Process.

Read and reread this chapter. There are lots of suggestions for using the process in depth. Over a period of time, as you use the Psychic Intuitive Guidance Process again and again, you will be more positive about life and have more trust in your intuition and in your connection to the Supreme Power of your understanding.

Let us use the experience of a woman named Vicky, and take a look at how she is using the Psychic Intuitive Guidance Process effectively.

Ask a Good Question and Write It Down

Vicky is having problems with a friend of hers. Her first step is to write a few statements about the situation and then ask a question. If Vicky preferred, she could also process this in her mind without writing anything down. I recommended that she write down her thoughts as she worked with the process, because it would be easier for her to be clear about her thoughts, and she would also have a record of her thoughts that she could refer to later.

Vicky began by writing a few statements about the situation and then asked a question.

> *Situation:* I am having a problem with a friend of mine. She keeps asking me to do favors for her, and the things she asks me to do are really things she should be doing for herself.

> *Vicky's Question:* How much should I help my friend? What Energy and State of Being do I need at this time to empower me to respond positively in this situation for the highest good of my friend and myself?

Vicky has stated the situation, and she has asked a question that relates to the situation. Vicky is obviously feeling like she needs to handle the situation with her friend better. It seems clear that Vicky has not yet stood up to her friend and refused to do things that her friend should really be doing for herself.

Vicky has been honest with herself about her feelings, and she clearly knows that she is helping her friend too much. She is also beginning to tune into her own inner wisdom by asking which Energy and State of Being she needs at this time.

Choose an Energy and a State of Being Intuitively

Vicky goes into a state of deep relaxation and tries to clear her mind of as much as possible. She is familiar with the Twelve Energies and the Four States of Being. As she uses her intuition, she tries hard not to make a logical decision, but to listen intuitively for the Energy that will empower her and then for the State of Being.

As she listens she hears, "The Communicator." Her logical mind told her that she would hear, "The Nurturer-Retreat From," but that is not what her intuition is leading her to. She writes down "The Communicator."

Next she listens for the State of Being that she needs to combine with the Energy of the Communicator. She hears, "Birth and Creation."

Vicky turns to page 69 to find the page number of the Communicator-Birth and Creation message. She sees that the message is on page 100. She turns to that page and reads the message while listening to the track of the Communicator on the CD.

Read the Message and Listen to the Music

Vicky reads the message and listens to the track on the CD that goes with the message. She is touched by the whole message, but particularly by one passage:

> The way I express myself no longer suits me. While the very heart and soul of what I call "myself" has transformed, I am still expressing myself in terms of the old me. I still talk the same way, walk the same way, and gesture the same way. My physical and mental bodies have not yet caught up with the changes of my inner spirit, my soul.

I am asking the Creator of All That Is to create within me new forms of expression, and I am receiving. I ask that I may integrate within my being all that is part of my being.

Be Open to Hearing What Your Psychic Intuitive Guidance Is Telling You

Vicky knows that she is not being honest with her friend. She has not been communicating with her friend totally honestly because up until this moment, she has not had the courage to say what is in her heart. This is not a new problem for Vicky. In this moment, as she receives the message and the music, she is admitting to herself that she has always had a hard time standing up to people if it meant saying "No." In this moment, the words that she reads in the message of the Communicator-Birth and Creation are helping Vicky to face the fact she needs to grow in her ability to express herself.

By choosing the Communicator-Birth and Creation, Vicky is receiving new energy for communicating. She is changing in this moment as she receives Divine help. As she listens to the music, the vibrations of change flow within her being.

Vicky writes the following reaction to this experience of using the Psychic Intuitive Guidance Process:

I am tired of walking around feeling a need to tell my friend that she has to take care of herself. I am really enabling her and I need to tell her that I am not doing her any favors by taking care of her the way I am. I also need to remind myself that all the energy I am putting into this friend needs to be applied to my own life and my own problems. As I have read the message and listened to the music, something has touched my heart. I feel very blessed and know that from this moment forward I am going to be able to express myself more honestly to people.

Vicky has used the Psychic Intuitive Guidance Process effectively. It has been a motivational and spiritual experience for her. She has stated the situation and asked a good question about her relationship to her friend. Next she used her intuition to choose an Energy and a State of Being that can empower her in her relationship with her friend. She has completed the process by reading the message, listening to the music, and writing down her thoughts as a result of the experience. The answers are clearly within Vicky, and she has accessed these answers and feels empowered as she never has before.

Now let's look at another experience with the Psychic Intuitive Guidance Process.

Amy was worried about her productivity level at work. She knew that promotions were going to be given within about six months, and she wanted a promotion. So she decided to use the Psychic Intuitive Guidance Process to empower herself.

Amy's Question: How can I be more productive at work?

Logically speaking, as Amy asked a question about being productive at work, she might say to herself, "The Energy that I need is the Producer." And again, if Amy stayed in a logical frame of mind, she might also decide that Moving Toward is the State of Being that she would want to apply to the Energy of the Producer. It would make sense that she would want to choose an Energy that relates to being productive and Moving Forward and into that Energy so that she could get more work done and have a better chance at getting a promotion at work.

But Amy knew that it was important to remember that when using one's psychic intuitive guidance, one is not trying to tap into one's logical ideas. Amy understood that if all she wanted was a logical solution she did not need to use her psychic intuitive guidance. She could easily figure out a way to make herself work harder. But something inside Amy called to her and let her know that there was more to this situation than just making a decision to work harder.

Amy listened within to hear what Energy and State of Being she needed at this time. What she heard was, "The Peacemaker." Next Amy asked, "What State of Being do I need to apply to the Energy of The Peacemaker?" What she heard was "Retreating From."

So now Amy had the combination Peacemaker-Retreating From. This was not a combination that she would have reached logically. She turned to page 69 to find the page number of the message that goes with that combination.

When she read the message and listened to the music on the CD, some of the words in the message quickly got Amy's attention. Here are the words:

> As I am taking an honest look at my behavior, I realize I am creating an atmosphere where no real peace can take place. I am smoothing over situations where people should have open discussions in order to bring their feelings out into the open.

As Amy read these words in the message and listened to the music, she suddenly flashed on an experience she had been having over and over at work. She had an image of two people in her department who are out to get each other. She thought about the ways that these two people are devious and lie to each other. Suddenly, as these images came into Amy's mind, she had a life-changing realization. She understood that she had been spending a lot of her precious time and energy at work acting as a peacemaker between these two people, and it has been sapping her energy and lowering her productivity. It had never occurred to her that the energy she was spending trying to keep them from arguing was part of what has been making her get less work done lately. But when she allowed herself to tap into her inner wisdom, she was led to the exact message that she needed to read that would jog her mind into realizing how she was wasting her energy at work.

Amy might never have realized what her real problem was if she had approached her problem using logic only. Logically telling herself to work harder would not have uncovered the deeper problem. But as she used the Psychic Intuitive Guidance Process, her intuition led her to read a message and listen to music that provided her with an opportunity to have images come to mind that led to her understanding of the deeper issues. Amy realized how she was wasting her energy at work.

Amy's story is a great example of how the conscious mind cannot find answers that the subconscious intuitive mind can find.

You may ask, "But what if I ask a question about being productive at work, and I really feel the Producer is the Energy I need at this time?"

It is also important to note that *if* your intuition rather than your logical thinking leads you to the Energy of the Producer and any of the States of Being that you might apply to that Energy, then of course that is what you need. You may also ask, "How can I know if my logical mind is choosing an Energy and State of Being or if I have tuned into my Psychic Intuitive Guidance?"

There is a difference in the quality of how you feel when you are thinking logically and when you are tuning into your intuitive guidance. When I am thinking logically, I feel very alert and organized. When I am tuning into intuitive guidance, I am often in a meditative, altered state of consciousness. I feel a bit dreamy.

You will have to experiment and learn to understand and sense when you are thinking logically and when you are tuning into another part of yourself that you are not always in touch with. Over time you will come to understand when you are really hearing or sensing guidance. It is a very special feeling, and I believe you will know when it is happening.

Some More Advice

After you've read the message and listened to the music that goes with that message, you may continue to receive guidance about your situation for the next several hours or even the next few days.

Get Rid of Preconceived Ideas

If you have a preconceived idea about what the answer to your question is, it will be hard for you to tap into your intuitive guidance. There is a natural psychic ability that is part of each one of us. Some of us feel more comfortable using that ability than others. It is that psychic ability that makes it possible for us to know when someone is going to call us on the telephone. It is that psychic part of us that knows we are going to see someone soon whom we have not seen for a long time, and that person shows up the next day. That same psychic ability brings us into alignment with our intuitive guidance. Try to clear your mind of any preconceived ideas about what the answer to your question will be or how you will react to the experience of reading the message and listening to the music. If you let go and see what happens, you may find that you will have many transformative experiences. As you continue to work with the Psychic Intuitive Guidance Process, your life will be improving.

Allow Yourself to Evolve Spiritually

It is my belief that as each one of us evolves spiritually, the guidance we receive reflects the level of consciousness to which we have evolved. I believe that our consciousness connects us with the Divine, and as we open up to listening to guidance from our inner voice, we will receive that which we are able to listen to.

There is an old expression: "When the student is ready the teacher will appear." We have to be ready to receive wisdom. It will not be given to us if we are not ready to receive it. If we are not willing to listen, why would the Creator send answers to deaf ears?

One of the gifts of working with the Psychic Intuitive Guidance Process is the opportunity to learn to listen to our inner voice. As we learn, we change and grow. As you and I strengthen our ability to listen to our inner guidance, our lives will transform and continue to transform.

You Have the Answers within Yourself

The answers are within you. You are using the Psychic Intuitive Guidance Process as a means of creating an emotional, psychological, and spiritual environment in which you are able to hear your inner wisdom. You will be forever changed by the experiences you have with this process. While you will continue to consult with experts and friends when it is needed, you will have more trust in your own ability to solve problems and live a positive life.

Chapter 11

USING THE PSYCHIC INTUITIVE GUIDANCE PROCESS WITH A FRIEND OR INTUITIVE READER

O nce you are familiar with the Psychic Intuitive Guidance Process and have used it by yourself, you may enjoy using the process with a friend, or you may want to seek the advice of an intuitive reader.

Using the Process with a Friend

Two People, Each Taking Turns
The two people working with this process may intuitively choose the same Energy and State of Being, or they make different choices. They are not to discuss their choices, but each is to tune in on an intuitive level and write down their choice without the other person seeing what they have chosen.

- Decide who is going to be the first to ask a question. We will call this person the Primary Person. The other person will be called the Secondary Person.

- The Primary Person describes a situation and then asks a question.

- The Primary Person uses her intuition to choose the Energy and State of Being needed at this time. She writes her choice down without showing it to the Secondary Person.

- The Secondary Person tunes in on the question asked by the Primary Person and asks what Energy and State of Being is needed at this time. She writes her choice down without showing it to the Primary Person.

- The Primary Person reads the message she has chosen while listening to the music on the CD.

- The Primary Person describes the experience she has had with the message and the music to the Secondary Person.

- The Secondary Person reads the message that she has chosen to the Primary Person. Both people listen to the message with the question of the Primary Person in mind. In other words, the Secondary Person is going to add additional input to the session.

- The Secondary Person speaks inspirationally about the experience she has had with the message and the music in relationship to how the wisdom that is coming through can help the Primary Person.

- Both parties now discuss the experiences they have both had with the process of addressing the Primary Person's question.

• Next, the two people change roles and repeat the process. The person who was the Primary Person now takes on the role of the Secondary Person and vice versa.

Two People, Only One Person Asks a Question

There may be occasions where only one person wants to ask a question. For instance, if one person is having a difficult time, the two people may want to focus on that person and not change roles and go through the process a second time. For instance, if your friend is seriously upset due to a divorce, the loss of a job, or any other serious situation, it may not be a time for you to trade sessions. You may need to only use the process for your friend that day. Or if you are seriously upset, you might want to ask your friend to do an intuitive guidance session for you, and reciprocate at another time when you are feeling better.

Using the Process with an Intuitive Reader

While Psychic Intuitive Guidance Process has been developed for you to use on your own or with a friend, you can also use the process in a session with an experienced and qualified intuitive reader. I use the process with my own clients. The difference between using this product on your own or with a friend and having a session with an experienced intuitive reader is that an intuitive reader has had years of experience working with clients and may bring extra and special guidance as you are working with the process. While you are tuning into your own inner guidance, the reader will also tune in for you and bring her wisdom to the experience. Your work with the process will be doubly beneficial as both you and the professional intuitive reader work together. My goal for my clients is that ultimately they will not need to see me very often because they will have the confidence and skills to tap into their own inner resources.

A Psychic Intuitive Guidance Session is not like a typical psychic reading where a psychic tells you what to do. In the Psychic Intuitive Guidance Session, you are empowered to delve deep and find your own answers. As a professional reader works with you, she will add her own insights to whatever situations you are addressing in your life. The session is much more interactive than the typical psychic reading, where the reader does most of the talking.

Neither is a Psychic Intuitive Guidance Session a mediumistic reading. When a medium (often called a "psychic medium") gives a reading, he is communicating with those who have passed over and is bringing their messages. The reading is not so much about you as it is about those who have passed over. It is possible that some of those who communicate from the world of spirit will give you advice about your current life situations, but it is just as possible that they will come in just to send their love and say hello.

To give you some examples of how clients use the Psychic Intuitive Guidance Process in a session with me, I would like to tell you about several sessions I've had with clients. What is important about each of these sessions is the *deep experience* that each person has. While we can access many answers to our problems logically, when we tune into our intuitive guidance, the answers become a transforming experience and the result is real inner change. People become empowered to have more successful lives when they learn to access their inner guidance.

Linda

Linda came to see me one day for a Psychic Intuitive Guidance session. I had sent her a copy of this book and CD prior to our appointment, so she was familiar with the Twelve Energies and the Four States of Being.

I explained to Linda that I feel called to work with clients in a way that empowers them to tune into their own inner wisdom. I explained that I act as a facilitator during the session, to help clients listen to their own inner voice. I promised that in the second half of the session, I would add my thoughts about whatever question she had asked and would also record an inspirational meditation related to her question that she could use at home.

Before starting the process and asking a question, Linda described a bit about her life: "I am a middle-aged woman with a grown daughter named Marilyn who is married to a man named Steven. They have two children. I am divorced and spend most of my time working at a job I really enjoy. However, I am unhappy about my relationship with my daughter. I find that she only calls me when she needs something, and expresses very little interest in what is going on in my life. Sometimes my feelings are hurt."

Linda's Question: How can I remain close to Marilyn without feeling judgmental and needy because Marilyn now has a family and does not always give me the attention I would like to have?

I asked Linda to quiet herself again and look at the names of the Twelve Energies and to choose the Energy she felt drawn to.

Linda's Energy: The Soloist

Then I asked Linda to consult with her intuitive guidance and tell me if she felt she needed to *move forward* and into the Energy of the Soloist, *retreat from* this Energy, ask for a new *birth and creation* of the Energy, or simply be *still in the essence of* the Energy of the Soloist. I told her not to try to figure it out logically, but just tell me which of the Four States of Being she felt drawn to.

Linda's State of Being: Birth and Creation

We turned to page 67 and found the page number for the message and the track number for the CD. We turned on the music and

Linda read the message out loud:

> New comfort is needed. I need to be more comfortable being alone. I am ready. I now take another step in my path of solitude.
>
> In this moment, I ask the Creator of All That Is to create a new energy for the part of me that is the Soloist. I pray that I may become more comfortable being alone. I pray that I may become more accepting of myself. It is my desire to stop running away from myself so that I will be more willing to create time in my life to be alone.
>
> Being alone can sometimes produce fear and anxiety. Being alone can sometimes make me feel like I am missing out on life. But without time alone, I become overwhelmed with the energy of other people.
>
> I often feel the need for others around me but then become overwhelmed with so many things going on at the same time: too many people, too many problems, too many opinions.
>
> *Stop turning from mirrors,* my soul calls to me. Love yourself as you are. "It is only in being with yourself that you can truly find your hearts desire."
>
> As I listen to the music of the Soloist, I feel new vibrations penetrating my being: vibrations of self-acceptance and ease of being with myself. In this moment, I know that as I spend more time alone I will become closer to my own being. I will become my own best friend.
>
> I listen to the music and let go of all tension. I accept a new creation of the Soloist Within. The voices of my soul weave the harmony of new creation.

Linda was visibly moved as she read the message out loud and listened to the music. Tears came to her eyes. After a few minutes of silence Linda said, "I ought to concentrate on me, not them."

This was a simple statement, but profound for Linda in this moment. She embraced a simple truth: she cannot focus so much energy on her grown daughter. She has to adjust to the change in her relationship with her daughter now that her daughter has a family and has moved away from the town where Linda lives.

Then Linda said, "I don't always have to explain to my daughter about the way I am feeling. I can just practice breathing in and out and saying that the way I feel about myself does not depend on how she is treating me. If she is calling me only when she needs something and is not treating me very well, I am in charge of my life and can decide whether I will put up with being treated badly or not. Some days it may feel okay to listen to her problems and fill her requests for money and other days it may not feel okay. On a day when it does not feel okay, I may have to say "No" to her requests and limit the amount of time we are on the phone. And if I am feeling really upset with her, there may be times I do need to tell her how I feel and then let it go. I can decide in each instance how I want to deal with her. I need to focus on my own life more. I need to learn to put my worry about her aside. She is an adult."

I asked Linda if there were any particular words in the message that seemed to jump off the page at her. She said that there were a couple of phrases that had a big impact on her: "New comfort is needed"; "Stop turning from mirrors. Love yourself as you are."

Linda went on to say that as she faced the fact that she would not be spending as much time with her daughter, it was forcing her to live with herself and be happy with herself. She told me that she was coming to understand that she had to feel good about herself even if she had no one around her to pat her on the back and tell her how great she was.

I asked Linda if there were any actions she wanted to take in her life as a result of her experience. I told her that what was most important were her reactions to the message and the music. I said that the ultimate guidance is not in the message or the music, but within her, and that the message and the music had simply acted as catalysts to help her listen to her own inner voice.

Linda said, "I want to spend more time meditating every day. I want to spend more time meditating or praying with the Buddhist breathing in breathing out. I have been doing this with Marilyn and Steven in mind, but now I want to do it with myself in mind."

The session concluded as I went into a state of deep inspiration. I played the music of the Soloist on the CD. The following words came through for Linda to say in her daily meditation. I recorded the inspiration for her.

Inspiration for Linda

I am Linda a soul from afar
Descended into this body for the span of my lifetime.
My life is my own and while my children are part of my
*   life, they are not my life.*
They are souls with their own paths and own callings.
There will be phases in life in which they cling to me and
*   other times when they go off for awhile.*
The love I have for my daughter is always and her love for
*   me is always.*
Sometimes the physical vehicle of one who is married goes
*   off for a while, but the love of her soul is always with*
*   me forever.*
This is a time to focus on the soul that is Linda.
There are dimensions of my own life that have been let go
*   during this time of focusing so much on her.*
This time now is for me and for the unfoldment of aspects
*   of my being I have never known before.*

*I will not look back at this time, but fly forward into the
unknown mysteries of my own existence.*
*I am not alone. I am always in the care of the Divine as is
my daughter.*

I wished Linda well and asked if she had any questions before we
concluded our time together. Linda asked, "How did you get the
words you just spoke to me? You said it was 'an inspiration' but
where does it come from?"

I told Linda that my inspirational words came from the part
of me that connects with my own psychic intuitive guidance. I also
said that I felt that each one of us connects with the Creator of the
universe and that we can receive guidance. I went on to say that
Linda had received her own guidance during the session from the
same source within herself.

We both thanked each other for the session. We also said a
prayer of thanks to the Creator for being part of the work that we
had done.

The Special Aspect of Linda's Session: Linda has realized that she
has to value herself more. This is a thought that is very common,
but in this case it is *not* the thought that is important; it is Linda's
experience of this concept on a very deep and spiritual level that
makes it a special experience. Linda could say the words "I need
to value myself," but just saying the words does not have the same
impact as the experience she has had with the message and the
music. She has been moved deeply.

Cindy

Cindy is a good friend whom I have known for more than twenty
years. I invited her to do a Psychic Intuitive Guidance Session with
me. She had been hearing about the book and CD as I was

developing this process, and she was excited to do the session. She read the book and listened to the CD prior to her session.

Cindy's Question: I had shingles recently, which was triggered by stress. How can I reduce stress in my life?

I asked Cindy to allow her psychic intuitive guidance to tell her which of the Twelve Energies and which of the Four States of Being she needed in this moment. Cindy was drawn to the Producer-Birth and Creation.

When Cindy made her choices, I felt very nervous. While I did not say anything to Cindy, I thought to myself that if she wanted to relax, asking for a new birth and creation of the Energy of the Producer did not seem to fit. After all, the Producer is an Energy of activity and production, and I would have thought that she might have been drawn to Retreating From the Energy of the Producer. *Then I realized that this was my logical mind speaking to me, and that I was making the same mistake I warned all my clients about.* I kept my mouth shut and waited to see what would happen. Here, I said to myself, was a real test of the Psychic Intuitive Guidance Process. Cindy had made her choice intuitively, and we would now see what that psychic part of herself was leading us to as we read the message and listened to the music. If the process was working, a choice that did not seem logical would turn out to be the best choice possible. Because Cindy is one of my best friends, I was anxious as we turned to page 68 to get the page number for the message of the Producer-Birth and Creation.

Cindy read the message out loud as she listened to the music of the Producer.

She got very excited and said that one sentence really jumped out at her: "Accomplishing my goals feels right in step with my everyday breathing and movement."

Cindy said, "What this phrase said to me is that if a person relaxes and works hard, it will not be exhausting if the person moves and breathes with the rhythm of what is being done. In other words, if one has a relaxed attitude, a lot of work can be done with a minimum of stress.

"What I want to do is to stop tuning into the outside world's expectation of me and do more of what I feel like inside. It feels like that would be energizing and positive and less stressful. It feels like it would be a good way to tap into my energy without depleting myself. It is funny how we have this intuitive sense about what is right for us but we don't always listen to it. Doing a process like this helps to tune into it."

Inspiration for Cindy

Life is all rhythm.
Life is all change.
As you dance to the rhythm of your own breath your life
  flows easily and effortlessly.
You do not need to stop doing as much
You need to flow with what you are doing
And as you do so, your energy will increase and increase
  and increase.

The Special Aspect of Cindy's Session: Cindy had an insight as she realized that it was *she* who was bringing stressful thoughts and vibrations to her life. She realized it was not her schedule, but her attitude that needed changing.

David

David told me why he had made an appointment: "I was feeling down and I thought perhaps something could happen during this session that would put me in a better mood." I asked David to relax and let a question come to him. He sat for a few minutes and then told me his question.

David's Question: Why do I wake up in the morning often feeling depressed?

David had read the book and was familiar with the Twelve Energies and the Four States of Being. I asked him to allow his intuition to tell him which Energy and which State of Being he needed.

David's Energy: The Communicator. "I don't know why, but I just feel drawn to that Energy more than any of the others."

David's State of Being: Retreating From

David and I turned to page 68 and found the page number for the message: The Communicator-Retreating From. We turned on the CD to play the music of the Communicator while reading the message.

Here are the words that jumped out at David as he read the message:

Have I been talking too much? Yes, I have. Not only are the people in my life tired of hearing me, but also I am tired of hearing my own voice. While I know that expressing my thoughts and feelings is important, right now my life is out of balance. It's funny how all great things live on a fine line. There is a fine line between not expressing myself enough and expressing myself too much. It is often hard for me to find that fine line. When I find it, my relationships are very comfortable and enjoyable. When I express myself too little, I feel all cooped up inside and separated from those I love. And then when I express myself too much, as I have lately, I feel exhausted, as do my loved ones who have been listening to me.

David said, "My God, I am complaining all the time and starting to believe in my own complaints. I really need to shut off all this negative talk!"

I asked David if there were any deep problems bothering him. Did he need to see a psychological counselor? He said, "No, I don't have any deep problems at this time. I think I have just become emotionally lazy. I want the world handed to me on a silver platter, and I complain when everything does not go just the way I want it to go."

I told David that happens to the best of us, and I would be eager to hear what happened to him over the next several months as he focused on complaining less and being happier more of the time.

Next I relaxed and went into a state of inspiration. I played the music of the Communicator and the following words came through, which I recorded and gave David to use as an inspirational meditation.

Inspiration for David

Here I am in an ocean of life.

I can sink or swim, as I like.

Sometimes the waters are calm and flow in a comfortable pattern

Sometimes the waves knock me around a bit and I am tired

But I am swimming in the ocean of life and know that the waters will always support me.

Life will support me one way or another.

I can choose to enjoy the swim or flail around in a state of frenzy.

It is always my choice

Always my choice.

The Special Aspect of David's Session: To put it bluntly, David realized that he was complaining too much. He made a decision to shut up about his problems and have a better life!

Kate

Kate arrived for her session with a moody expression on her face. She told me that she was a floor manager in an exclusive retail store and that four of her best employees had decided to quit and go to work for another store. Kate had been training these people for a while and really thought she was building a great team. When four of her best got together and decided they would rather work someplace else, it really hurt. To make matters worse, Kate was on a business trip abroad when these four gave notice. When she returned to the store, they were already gone. In the weeks to come, none of them called to say good-bye or to express their appreciation for the way that Kate had really worked hard to make them the best sales people ever.

I asked Kate what question she would like to ask in relationship to the experience she had just described to me.

> *Kate's Question*: I feel hurt and abandoned. What will make me feel better?

> *Kate's Energy*: The Warrior

> *Kate's State of Being*: Still in the Essence Of

As Kate read the message and listened to the music of the Warrior, these are the words that jumped out at her:

> When I am able to take life as it comes, and accept that I cannot control everything that happens, I am able to live a life both rich and spiritual. Even though there is much in my life that I can control, there are many circumstances

that are unexpected. If I try to control every minute of my life it is not possible and a waste of my precious energy.

I am the Warrior as I am able to take life as it comes and do the best I can with whatever life brings my way. I turn to the Warrior Within to cope with anything that happens.

Kate said that as she read the message she realized that she is often upset when things happen that are unexpected. She said, "I know that I would like to control what happens. I wanted so much to build this team at work, and when it fell apart I also fell apart."

I asked Kate if there were any actions she wanted to take as a result of the experience she had had with the message and the music. Kate replied, "I want to concentrate on three words in the message: *my precious energy.* I want to remember that life is short, and that unexpected things happen all the time and will continue to happen for the rest of my life. I want to work with myself to become more flexible. I don't want to spend my time brooding over things that happened yesterday. I want to learn to move on in life knowing that each day is a new day."

At the end of the session, I went into a state of inspiration and the following words came through for Kate to use in her meditations:

Inspiration for Kate

I am Kate and I am Kate no matter who is with me or who leaves my side.

I am Kate and I can handle any situation that comes along.

I am more flexible than I ever was before.

I respond more easily to unexpected situations.

I am Kate and I like myself!

This inspirational message stuck both of us as a bit funny. We both laughed out loud. Kate left our session in a great mood. I also felt great, as the messages of the Warrior and the music are always uplifting.

The Special Aspect of Kate's Session: Kate realized that in business, she could not get so personally involved with her employees. She had to accept that people would come and go. She also felt the strength of the Warrior within her and that she could handle any situation that life threw at her.

Roger

Roger entered the session with a lot of enthusiasm, eager to get some answers! He promptly explained his situation: "My question has to do with relationships, interpersonal relationships. I have often been told or have felt that I am a loner, and I have this sense that I am a loner. I am comfortable being by myself."

> *Roger's Question*: What should I do when I need to interact on a very personal and intimate basis with another person?

> *Roger's Energy*: The Nurturer

> *Roger's State of Being*: Birth and Creation

Roger sat back in his chair, and as he listened to the music and read the message his whole body seemed to relax.

I asked Roger if there were any words in the message that seemed to jump off the page.

"Yes," he replied. "The words that jump out at me are, "I am tired of nurturing myself," and "I need new energy at this time."

Roger went on to say, "I want to feel that the vibrations in the music can be helpful. I want the music to spark a new creation of the Nurturer and give me a new lease on life. I want to receive motivation to continue the search within myself. I want a sense of comfort that the search will be successful. I want to believe that with a burst of new energy, I can have better relationships."

Then Roger said, "I guess having the trust in myself that I am strong enough to go forward and succeed is most important. I have to believe that I can be intimate with another person. I realize I have tended to be anxious when I am interacting with someone else, and I need to get rid of that anxiety. I need to express myself. I also need to listen to the other person and have more of an understanding of where that person is coming from."

As Roger spoke, I noticed that he never used the name of this "other person." I knew that he was in a serious relationship with a young woman, and I suspected he was talking about her. But I did not say anything. I just listened.

Roger continued, "I must admit that as I open up, I am somewhat afraid of the unknown in terms of where opening up may lead. I do not know what will happen. But I understand that it is more important to go forward than it is to sit in silence and potentially keep either myself or the other person from living life to the fullest.

"I need to open up. I guess I am troubled because I haven't been able to deal with this, even while recognizing its importance both to me and to someone else. My recollection is of letting myself be 'stepped on' or at least feeling that way and choosing to withdraw rather than to face up to it. I need to speak up when I feel stepped on."

I asked, "Why do you think you picked the Nurturer?"

Roger responded, "As I looked at the Energies, that one seemed to mean more. It seemed to mean more about the type of person I am and also what I enjoy doing, which is providing nurture and support, being helpful, and trying to understand a person within a given context. I try to provide encouragement regardless of whether or not that seems to be understood or appreciated."

I replied, "It's interesting that you chose the Nurturer, which you associate with being helpful to people, and yet all of your early descriptions of yourself are of being a loner. It is as if both qualities reside in you, and perhaps it is balance you are seeking."

Roger continued, "I have tended to put someone else before myself. I feel that I am a good number two person to someone else I enjoy being with. I do not usually take the lead in a situation but would prefer to be the facilitator, the implementer, and the supporter."

As the session came to an end, I could see that Roger was in conflict about who he was. As he tuned into his psychic intuitive guidance, he realized he did want to be closer to people. He wanted to get to know people better, especially the woman in his life, and he wanted people to know him better. He also realized that he felt stepped on sometimes, and in order to feel better, he needed to speak up.

Inspiration for Roger

You have to live with yourself.

You were born with yourself and you will die with yourself as your spirit makes its way to the world beyond.

You speak of being a number two person, always assisting and helping to facilitate the projects of others.

Value your work as a number two person

But consider the possibility of being a number one person on some projects also.

Life is not rigid.

Roles can be flexible.

So while in one situation you play number two role, in another situation you play number one person.

Be your own project.

Ask those around you to help you.

Let someone else play the number two role for you.

Life is vital

Life is creative

*Life can be as flexible or as rigid as we choose to make it.
What do you choose?*

The Special Aspect of Roger's Session: Roger realized that while
he had been nurturing people for a long time, he was not really
open with them emotionally. He was always putting others before
himself, and while he thought of this as a good and nurturing
thing to do, he was beginning to resent the fact that he always felt
like the second fiddle in the orchestra. My hope is that Roger will
find balance in his life. He will continue to play the role of the
Nurturer, which comes naturally to him, but he will also open up
and express himself. He will be as sensitive and nurturing to himself as he has always been to others.

We can learn a lot from each client session presented in this chapter. I am struck by the bravery each person showed as he or she
was willing to take a leap of faith and do an intuitive reading.
Each client was able to use his or her psychic energy to lead to a
message in the book that brought answers to questions and new
ideas to think about. As I do intuitive readings for myself and
watch others use the process, I am always amazed that there is a
part of us that we are not conscious of, yet that knows which message we need to read.

I was also impressed by the way the clients reacted to the messages they read and the music they listened to. Certain words and
phrases in the message acted as catalysts and stimulated them into
facing the truth about themselves and whatever situation they
were trying to deal with. I watched each client delve deep into
their inner wisdom as they became more and more honest with
themselves.

Every time I use the Psychic Intuitive Guidance Process with a
client, I learn something about life.

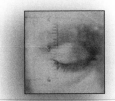

YOU KNOW WHAT YOU NEED

I believe in you.
You know what you need.
While others can be helpful and you need their guidance,
*   it is your body, mind and spirit that ultimately know*
*   what you need.*
Trust yourself.
Cultivate a deep friendship with your inner wisdom.
Know that you have a higher self that is part of All Divine
*   Wisdom.*

You are energy
You are vibration
You are a complex bundle of talents.

Each talent has a special energy and vibration of its own.
Call on the various parts of yourself, as you need to.
You always have options and let your psychic intuitive
*   guidance repeat the options again and again.*

You are powerful.
Never give your power away.
You are in charge of your life.

No one can take care of you.
Ultimately the responsibility is yours.
You are it, like it or not.
It is more fun to like it.
Like yourself
Love yourself
Have a good time
Have a good life.
It is your choice.
Choice is your life
Choice
Choice
Choice.

Send in Your Stories

Share your experiences with the process with Carole Lynne.

I am interested in knowing how your life changes as you work with this book and CD. Please feel free to write to me with your stories. Include your name, address, and phone number. Also, if you are giving me permission to share your stories with others in seminars or articles, please include a letter that states you are giving me permission. Let me know if I should change your name or leave it the same.

Carole Lynne
P.O. Box 600183
Newton, MA 02460

About the Author

CAROLE LYNNE IS A PSYCHIC MEDIUM, author, musician, and motivational speaker. She gives demonstrations, performs spiritually oriented music, and teaches seminars on mediumship throughout the US and the UK. She is the author of *Heart and Sound* and *How to Get a Good Reading from a Psychic Medium* and the founder of Singing for the Soul®, a spiritual approach to singing, and Quality Performance Coaching, for performers and public speakers.

If you would like to schedule a Psychic Intuitive Guidance session or invite Carole Lynne to give a seminar contact her at:

Phone: 617 964-0058

Email: CaroleLynne777@aol.com or
CaroleLynne2003@yahoo.com

Visit her website at *www.carolelynne.com*.